Kelso Abbey

a Layman's Guide

KELSO
CAMEOS

Audrey Mitchell

ISBN 0 9531026 3 7

Published by Audrey Mitchell, 19 Forestfield, Kelso, Scottish Borders TD5 7BX. All rights reserved. No part of this book may be reproduced or transmitted in any form or by any means, electronic or mechanical, including photocoying, recording, or by any information storage and retrieval system without permission in writing from the publisher.

Printed in the Scottish Borders by Kelso Graphics.

Frontispiece:
Stained glass panel by Kelso artist, the late R. Macdonald Scott, which now adorns the principal room of Kelso's Town House. By kind permission of his widow, Mrs Anne Scott, and the Scottish Borders Council.

By the same author:

Kelso's Ragged School
James Dickson and his Legacy
Historic Kelso
A Borders Schoolmaster

for Mairi

Contents

Introduction

Kelso Abbey is of enormous importance, not only to the town which surrounds it and the people who regard it as central to their community, but to Scotland's history.

It was built when other similar edifices were springing up all over Europe and so ensured that the country was in the forefront of progress at that time. The founder, David I, King of Scots, of proud lineage, was a man of breeding and culture and highly regarded by his contemporaries. His legacy surrounds us today, particularly in the Borders, where Melrose and Jedburgh also have magnificent ruins for us to cherish. Following his monarch's example, the Constable of Scotland, Hugh de Morville, endowed another fine Abbey at Dryburgh.

Add to this the lofty ruin of David's castle at Roxburgh, so strategically important that it was the focus of much bitter fighting between Scots and English, and occupied by enemy forces so often that Kelso and its Abbey were subjected to continual warfare. While David lived, it was his favourite residence and reinforced his special affection for this area – illustrated by the fact that his beloved son Prince Henry was buried in Kelso Abbey.

Detailed descriptions of the Abbey have been written, usually concentrating on the architecture, and chapters about it are included in many a local history, so this book is not intended to be an academic study but rather an informative narrative about a subject dear to the heart of every Kelsonian.

Audrey Mitchell
Kelso, April 2001.

IMMEDIATE FAMILY CONECTIONS OF KING DAVID

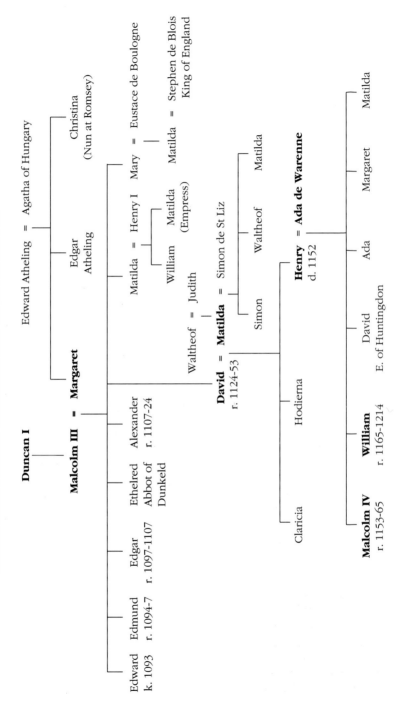

Chapter One

The Founder

ing David I (1124-1153) was born in 1084, a time when Norman influence was at its height. He was the sixth son of Malcolm III, King of Scots and his second wife, Margaret, who was later sanctified for her piety. When he was 9 years old David's parents both died, and to escape the turmoil of the power-struggle for succession to the Scottish throne, he was taken to England, where his sisters, Matilda and Mary, were living in a convent in Hampshire with their aunt Christina. William Rufus, son of William the Conqueror, was then in power and he supported David's brother Edgar in gaining the throne of Scotland. When William died in 1100 his brother Henry succeeded as king of England and the same year took David's sister Matilda (also known as Edith) as his Queen. Henry I seems to have favoured his young brother-in-law and made David Earl of Cumbria, with his headquarters at Carlisle Castle, for which David paid homage.

Queen Margaret had introduced the Roman Catholic faith into Scotland and gradually it superseded the old Celtic church. Margaret founded Dunfermline Abbey *(below)* and had a small oratory within Edinburgh Castle.

Her sons inherited her piety and Edgar granted the old church at Coldingham to the monks of Durham, who developed it into a Priory. He began the parish system in Scotland with a grant to Thor Longus of land at Ednam near Kelso, where a settlement – a "vill" – had a church built within it and conferred on the monks of St. Cuthbert. Edgar reigned for ten years but he was unmarried, had no direct heir and his nearest brother, Ethelred, was Abbot of Dunkeld and therefore ineligible to succeed. Before his death in 1107, Edgar decreed that his brother Alexander should reign over the Northern part of Scotland as King, with jurisdiction over

David as Earl in the Southern part. Alexander married Sibylla, a natural daughter of Henry I (his brother-in-law) but they had no children. Alexander continued the family's pious tradition by founding Inchcolm Abbey on an island in the Forth.

David, as Earl, founded a monastery in honour of St. Mary and St. John the Evangelist at Selkirk in 1113. He brought from Tiron, near Chartres in France, a group of monks from an order founded by Bernard, whose Rule was reformed Benedictine. He granted the monks many gifts of land, some from his earldom in England, and produce from fishings and mills. In 1114, at St. Peter's, Northampton, David married Matilda, widow of Simon de St. Liz and daughter of Waltheof, late Earl of Northumbria. Matilda's mother Judith was niece to William the Conqueror and cousin to Henry I. On David's marriage, Henry created him Earl of Huntingdon and as such he founded a monastery at Great Paxton on the Ouse.

When Alexander died in 1124 without a legitimate heir, David and Matilda became King and Queen of Scots. They had a son, Henry, and two daughters, Claricia and Hodierna, and with them spent a good deal of time at one of their main residences, Roxburgh Castle, across the Tweed from Kelso.

Distant view of Kelso across the Teviot from the ruins of Roxburgh Castle.

Four years after he became king, David decided to transfer the Tironensian Abbey which he had founded at Selkirk to a site in Kelso, having decided that the site at Selkirk was not suitable. Throughout his reign, David founded several other abbeys in Scotland which were manned by different Orders of monks. Melrose (1136) was Cistercian, and monks from this abbey were sent to Newbattle (1140 – founded by David and his son Henry), and to Kinloss (1150). Dundrennan (1142) in Kirkcudbrightshire was also Cistercian, but Holyrood (1128) Cambuskenneth (1140) and Jedburgh (1138) were Augustinian.

Henry I of England and his Queen Matilda had a son, William, who drowned in a shipwreck in 1120. Their daughter, also Matilda, married firstly Henry, the Holy Roman Emperor (and so was known as Empress Maud), and secondly Geoffrey Plantaganet. On the death of her father in 1135, Matilda became Queen of England but was challenged by her cousin Stephen. To complicate matters, Stephen was married to yet another Matilda, daughter of David's sister Mary who had married Eustace of Boulogne. David was therefore torn between his niece Matilda (Empress Maud) and the husband of his other niece, Matilda! England was rent by civil war and David became involved in the Battle of the Standard at Northallerton 1138, which ended in his defeat. Matilda and Stephen continued to fight for the throne until she left England in 1147.

By this time David was over 60 years old and planning to name his son Henry as heir to the throne. Unfortunately, Henry died in 1152 and his father arranged for him to be buried in Kelso Abbey, which was still only partially built. Henry had married Ada de Warenne, daughter of the Norman Earl of Surrey, and they had 6 children. Their eldest son Malcolm was named heir to the throne and given the traditional title of Earl of Strathclyde. He succeeded as Malcolm IV, King of Scots, when David died on 24th May 1153 at his castle in Carlisle.

Sources:

Scottish Abbeys – *Stewart Cruden*
A History of England – *Keith Feiling*
A Short History of Scotland – *Andrew Lang*
The Lion in the North – *John Prebble*
Making of the Nations – *Scotland* – *Robert Rait*
David the Prince – *Nigel Tranter*

Plan of Tiron Abbey

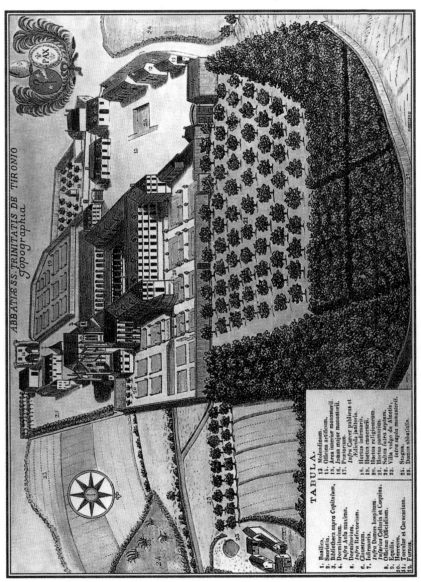

By kind permission of Denis Guillemin

Chapter Two

The Order

The monks invited by David to form his monastery at Kelso came from Tiron, near Chartres in France. Early in the 12th century, their leader, Bernard, a Benedictine monk, had arrived in Perche from Normandy with others seeking a hermitage. The castle of Nogent was occupied by Rotrou, Count of Perche, who was married to Matilda, an illegitimate daughter of Henry I of England. He gave Bernard ground in a small valley at Brunelles where his ancestors had founded an oratory, but Rotrou's mother feared that the monks at St. Denis of Nogent would object and the grant was revoked. The next gift was in the forest at Tiron where Bernard created a monastery from a wooden chapel surrounded by cabins, and Mass was celebrated here for the first time on Easter Day 1109 in the presence of Bishop Yves of Chartres. The monks at St. Denis were still unhappy so after five years Bernard was obliged to move and the little chapel of St. Anne des Bois now marks the spot where this wooden monastery stood. Rotrou gave Bernard a new site near the Tiron river, outwith the jurisdiction of St. Denis, and the donation was confirmed on 3rd February 1113. Bernard died in April 1116.

The Tironensian male community followed the Benedictine Rule as reformed by Bernard: a life of penitence and austerity, but with an emphasis on manual work and crafts in addition to prayer and Bible study. Wearing grey robes, (at Kelso they later wore black) they went to bed at 7 p.m. in winter, lay on mattresses of straw with one blanket to cover them and rose at 2 a.m. when bells summoned them to the Office of the Virgin. At 4.15 a.m. Matins were sounded and the monks recited the Office of the Dead for the benefactors of the Abbey. Later they gathered in a warming-room to hear a chapter of the Rule and receive lectures and instruction from the Abbot, then worked in silence until midday. Each monk followed his own art or skill and stone masons, blacksmiths, carpenters all worked together to create a beautiful edifice for worship, the sum of their combined efforts so much greater than their individual contributions. The service of Vespers at 6 p.m. was followed by supper and the day ended with another pious lecture, chanting and meditation.

Henry I of England, father-in-law of Rotrou, had a high regard for Bernard and was instrumental in spreading the influence of the Tironensians who were sought after by several prospective founders of abbeys in England, Wales and Scotland. In 1115, the Norman Robert Fitzmartin brought 12 monks to set up a Priory in St. Dogmaels in West Wales and endowed it with lands in Devon and Ireland. Four years later it was promoted to an Abbey at the instigation of the king.

Henry I was also father-in-law to Geoffrey d'Anjou (Plantaganet) who was second husband to heiress Princess Matilda. Both Geoffrey and Rotrou liberally supported the Abbey at Tiron, as did Henry's natural son, Robert of Gloucester. Thiboult, Count de Blois, father of Stephen who later became King of England, gave 5 sous of rent on the port of Blois. Henry's brother-in-law, David of Scotland, at that time an Earl, also invited twelve monks with a Prior to come from Tiron to Selkirk where he founded an Abbey. David's father Malcolm III had built a castle at Selkirk with a manor known as the *villa regis*, and this new site became the *villa abbatis*.

The first Abbot of the monastery at Selkirk was Radalphus, followed by William who became Abbot of Tiron 1119 – 47. Herbert the 3rd Abbot of Selkirk was in post when the monastery was transferred to Kelso in 1128.

The **Abbot** was at the head of each community, father of the monks, and presided over all important decisions, nominated the various office-bearers and took full responsibility. The Abbot visited dependent abbeys and priories or invited their leaders to come to him. At Pentecost each year all Tironensian Abbots gathered at the Chapter General in Tiron except the

Present doorway of Tiron Abbey.

Scots, English, and Welsh who attended every 3rd year. The Abbot of Tiron was seated centrally with the others, following tradition, to his right or left. This was an opportunity to discuss matters of administration or infringement of monastic discipline and the proceedings were recorded by a scribe. The duties of the Abbot were such that he seldom mingled with the monks, having a separate lodging where he could entertain important guests – the Abbot of Tiron had the use of a large town-house in Paris. In some instances, an Abbot was obliged to provide armed knights for the king's service

The **Prior** was deputy to the Abbot when the latter was absent, or took charge of a Priory when it was a satellite house to the Abbey. He was responsible for the day-to-day operation of the Abbey.

The **Sacristan** was in charge of the fabric of the church building, the holy vessels, fine linen, embroidered robes and banners for carrying in procession. He also supervised the cleanliness of the church, the rush flooring, wax for candles and oil for lamps. The **sub-Sacristan** was responsible for the bell-ringing, which was carried out several times a day to call monks to prayer, and ensured that there was heating for those who ministered at the altar.

The **Infirmarian** was in charge of the Abbey hospital. He and his assistants became skilled in the use of herbs from the garden for medicine and ointment, and in elementary surgery. They might earn some money by charging laymen for advice or treatment.

The **Almoner** distributed alms, food and clothing to the poor, who queued up at the door, and to pilgrims, lepers or beggars.

The **Hospitaller** received guests and pilgrims and ensured that they had a bed in the guest-house, usually gratis. It was a pious duty to look after travellers but a prolonged visit by nobility could be a costly affair.

The **Cellarer** had charge of the cellar of ales and wines and storerooms for food. He also arranged transport of goods by land or water, buying carts as well as victuals. At fair-time, the cellarer might buy luxuries such as fruit, sugar and spices. Monks were forbidden to eat meat, but could have poultry and eggs, fish from their ponds and vegetables from the garden.

The **Kitchener** obtained his rations from the cellarer and either cooked or supervised the cooking, sometimes for very large numbers. Eating was done in a refectory and the **Refectorian** saw to the laying of table and the serving of meals.

The **Chamberlain** provided the clothing and bedding for the monks. He made sure there was a supply of hot water for feet-washing on Saturdays and for the shaving of heads every three weeks. Baths were taken four or five times a year.

The **Precentor** or **Chanter** took charge of the music. Not everyone appreciated the variety of singing, for in the 12th century the monk Aelred of Rievaulx, who spent time in the court of King David, complained that monks were *"doing all sorts of ridiculous things, plaguing us with womanish falsettos, spavined bleating and tremelos....open mouths not so much singing as doing ludicrous feats of breathing so that they looked as if they were in their last agony or lost in rapture. Their lips are contracting, their eyes roll, their shoulders are shaken upwards and downwards, their fingers move and dance to every note."* The precentor also looked after the books, a treasured part of monastic life.

Monks sat at desks in alcoves called carrells usually situated on the north side of the cloisters in a **Scriptorium**. They used quills to copy out the Gospels or Psalms in manuscripts using colour for illustrated initial letters which were often illuminated.

Aspiring young monks joined as novices and were supervised by a master until they made their vows of chastity and obedience to God and the Abbot.

There was a hierarchy in the ecclesiastical world which was headed by the ***bishop*** who had charge of the diocese. (There were no *archbishops* in Scotland until the 15th century, when St. Andrews and Glasgow were elevated). The ***archdeacon*** supervised the diocese, or part of it, under the supervision of the bishop. The ***dean*** supervised a group of churches and the ***rector*** had one parish, receiving the tithes as revenue. The rector was often absent so he appointed a ***vicar***, who might have a ***curate*** as assistant.

In common with many other religious institutions, the enterprise at Tiron grew large and wealthy, losing sight of Bernard's altruistic philosophy. The monks had an incredible store of riches locked in the strong-room of the Abbey, including sumptuous vestments of silk, gold and silver; chalices; chandeliers; incense-holders; reliquaries; vases: many were encrusted with jewels. They owned considerable lands in the regions of Loire, Maine, Normandy and Ile de France including many Priories. From the time of the Reformation, Abbeys in France, like those in Scotland, were administered by Commendators, appointed by the king, who were not obliged to be resident there but could benefit from the revenues. Meanwhile, the monks who remained were governed by a Prior.

The Tironensian Abbey at St. Dogmaels was suppressed in 1536, Kelso was finally destroyed by English forces in 1545, and Tiron itself was sacked by a Protestant force 3,000 strong in 1562. The number of monks at Tiron was reduced to 15 while those at Kelso died out in 1587. Henri IV of France

The ruins of St. Dogmaels Abbey – Photograph by David and Ann Grainger.

appointed his natural son Henri de Bourbon-Verneuil as Abbot of Tiron in 1606 and he largely restored the Abbey and invited a group of monks who respected the Rule of St. Benedict to settle there. When Henri left after his marriage in 1668, he was followed by Jean-Casimir Vasa who had just abdicated the throne of Poland. Vasa's successor, Philipe de Lorraine, enhanced the abbey with tapestries and planted trees in the garden. There were several other Commendators until the title of Abbot was suppressed in 1782.

A military College was established beside Tiron Abbey in 1776 and the monks were assisted by lay teachers in educating the cadets. Napoleon Bonaparte obtained a bursary to study there but his father decided to send him to the military college in Brienne where the emphasis was on science and mathematics.

The French Revolution of 1789 brought an end to the monastic orders and the Abbeys, when religious estates were sold by auction. However, the military College brought growth to the burgh of Tiron and in 1790 it joined with a neighbouring burgh to become Thiron-Gardais.

Sources:

Scottish Abbeys – Stewart Cruden
Thiron, Abbaye Medievale – Denis Guillemin
St. Dogmael's Abbey – John B. Hillin
Scotland's Music – John Purser
Monasteries – R. J. Unstead
Christian Heritage in the Borders – John Dent & Rory McDonald

Plan of Kelso Abbey
as visualised by the author.

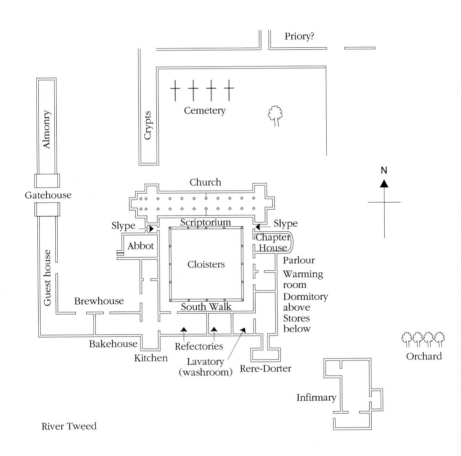

Priory?

Almonry

Crypts

Cemetery

Gatehouse

N

Church

Slype Scriptorium Slype

Abbot Chapter House

Guest house

Cloisters

Parlour

Warming room

Dormitory above

Stores below

Brewhouse

South Walk

Bakehouse

Kitchen

Refectories

Lavatory (washroom)

Rere-Dorter

Orchard

Infirmary

River Tweed

Chapter Three

The Buildings

bbeys of the twelfth century were built to a blueprint based on a plan of the Swiss Abbey of Saint Gall, and Benedictine Abbeys are grouped together in documents known as the Monasticon Gallicanum. Kelso Abbey was unusual in having an extra transcept but apart from that it is likely to have contained all the standard offices required for the smooth running of a monastery.

Building began on Kelso Abbey in the main church most likely with the East end, where the High Altar stood. Prince Henry was buried in 1152 when the Abbey had only existed for 25 years and such an important personage would surely be interred before the Altar. The cloister on its south side was also begun at this time. The West end is thought to have been built some 60 years later but adhered to the original Norman design. Excavations at the Abbey site have uncovered foundations of workshops and industrial and domestic debris dating from the 12th century while building work was proceeding. The stonework of the Abbey is of sandstone, pale grey to buff yellow in colour, which possibly came from a quarry at Sprouston, approximately 2.5 miles further down the Tweed. Because it is soft and inclined to crumble, the carvings have become worn and indistinct.

The West doorway (the partially surviving entrance which now faces Bridge Street) was the entrance through which processions of monks and dignitaries would pass. Walking through the Galilee porch you come to the Western crossing, above which the now silent Bell Tower still stands, with transcepts to North and South.

The West door from a print c.1845.

Leading to the North transcept is the doorway with pediment above, through which the ordinary townsfolk entered the Abbey. Beyond is the nave with aisles on either side, divided into three by the great pillars which once supported the wooden roof with its cover of leaden sheets. The highest rows of windows were known as the clearstorey, designed to admit as much light as possible, and a circulating passage along this level, and the one below, was reached by newel stairs in the angle-buttresses. The floor (as described in 1517) was partly paved and partly of bare earth. Along the sides were around a dozen small altars where monks and secular chaplains said mass daily.

The arrangement of windows giving internal light would have resulted in a fairly gloomy nave, but shafts of light passing through stained glass windows would have poured in at the site of the two crossings and must have been quite dramatic in effect. Add to that the brightly painted pillars, wall paintings, gilding and gleam from sacred vessels, rich vestments and cloths and you have a building vibrant with colour. Candles, usually made of beeswax, would have been used extensively, and in the early hours of a dark morning their flickering in the hands of black-robed, chanting monks must have been an eerie sight.

The total length of the Abbey was 302 feet: the length of the nave was divided in two by a wall which prevented the public from entering the Eastern end of the Abbey. On this wall was a platform on which stood the altar of the Holy Rood, an object of great veneration, and a tin organ. Aelred of Rievaulx was no more fond of organ music than of singing: *"Meanwhile the people standing, trembling and thunderstruck, wonder at the noise of the bellows, the clashing of bells and the harmony of pipes"*. In their outer section the parishioners could hear mass and receive sacraments from the parochial vicar. Beyond, the monks chanted and celebrated the Divine Office. Only at Divine Service could laymen enter, and women were never admitted except during church festivals.

The Abbey had its High Altar to the east for this was the direction facing Jerusalem, but it also satisfied a deep-rooted instinct in man to worship the daily sunrise. The choir was in the Eastern end with the High Altar and here several masses were celebrated daily, one for the Founder and others according to the particular festival. Above the choir was a second square Tower with pyramidal roof. To the right of the choir was the Sacristy where silver vessels and chalices were kept with a silver cross and other precious ornaments.

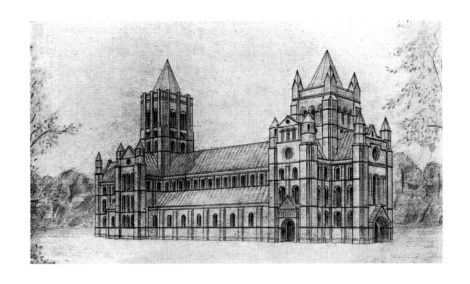

An interesting comparison of drawings of the Abbey elevation as presented by Henry F. Kerr (above) and A.F. Morse (below).

The vessels were washed in a **Piscina** situated to the south of the altar. In the stalls for the monks were seats known as **misericordes** consisting of a back with a folding seat which had underneath a carving, often executed by the monk himself.

A full description of the architectural features of the Abbey is contained in the volumes produced by the Royal Commission of the Ancient Monuments in Scotland. It is interesting to note that they draw attention to the asymmetrical section of the piers of the nave arcade as being similar to those of Romsey Abbey in Hampshire. This was where Christina, aunt of the Founder, David I, was a nun and where his sisters stayed before their marriage. Did some of the masons travel North with David?

Adjoining the gable of the South transcept is the outer **parlour** which was accessed by a doorway and had a passage (a **Slype**) connecting it with the **cloisters**, which at Kelso were on the South side of the Abbey stretching towards the Tweed, square and spacious around a green lawn. The covered walkways provided a sheltered place for walking and meditating and very likely the novices, sitting on stone benches, would have occupied a section while receiving tuition from their master. Young boys, sons of landowners, were also accepted as scholars. The northern side of the cloister against the cathedral wall, facing the sun, would probably have held the **Scriptorium**, where the monks painstakingly produced or copied illuminated manuscripts and other decorative works of theology.

Kelso had two **refectories**, or dining-halls, large and small, and the monks would eat in silence, presided over by the Abbot, Prior and seniors sitting on a dais. Adjacent was the kitchen where a fairly frugal meal was prepared – soup, eggs, fish, fruit and vegetables, mostly grown by themselves. Cooking would have been done in a cauldron or on a spit. Bread was baked in the bakehouse and the monks in Kelso would not have been short of ale. Before eating, the monks washed their hands in the washroom or **lavatory**. This was very necessary in days before cutlery was used and food was picked with the fingers from a trencher, which consisted of a thick slice of two-day-old bread. The **rere-dorters**, or toilets, were probably on the side nearest the river and the drainage system would take soiled water in this direction.

On another side of the cloister was the **Chapter-house** where the monks met daily to receive instruction from a senior – the Abbot or Prior. Any matters of discipline or confessions of wrongdoing were raised and punishment meted out. Other serious subjects involving charters, grants, purchases of land, perhaps disputes of tenants, were also heard here. The **library** may have been above the Chapter House – the religious orders were usually the only people who could read and write and were invaluable in this respect, recording events in chronicles.

The **dormitory**, with its individual cells and corridor, was usually sited above the **warming room** where monks could heat themselves in front of the only fire in the monastery, so the wood-store would be nearby. The **parlour** was the talking room (from the French parler) and here the monks, on rare occasions, could entertain their relatives and engage in conversation.

The Benedictine Rule laid importance on care of invalids, and there was an **infirmary** for the sick and infirm, with an apothecary in charge whose drugs and herbs would be well-guarded. The monks grew their own herbs, brewed potions and used beeswax, honey and other natural substance to make liniments. At Kelso, during excavation, quantities of pottery fragments of locally-made glazed jugs and plain, straight-sided cooking pots also from the 12th century were found in a pit beneath what was the infirmary hall and these may have been introduced by the monks. Evidence of stone and timber structures with a spread of stone chippings suggested a mason's lodge where builders lived and worked. An enormous pit 23 feet long was found which may have been a gravel quarry, containing pots which were probably used as back-fill when the infirmary was being built. The infirmary of Kelso Abbey was 53 feet wide and 106 feet long, with the length running North to South, and was likely to have been originally timber-built, replaced by stone. There were two parallel rows of pillar bases, alternately circular or octagonal, which ran along the building to create two aisles as wards for the sick. It would also have had a chapel, a nearby kitchen and possibly a house for the distribution of alms. A **Misericorde**, or room where the Rule was relaxed, was provided for resting. Monks were fond of being bled and this was done on a regular basis in the infirmary, the only time they were permitted a diet of meat. In addition to the infirmary, there was a "**Maisondieu**" not far from Roxburgh Castle where the diseased and the infirm were cared for.

Round a wide court were houses and lodgings, with quarters for guests, and the Abbey would have had a protective high wall all round, with a large Gate-house in the centre. Recent excavations during the building of flats on Bridge Street, between the Abbey and the river, uncovered foundations of buildings which are likely to have been the Kelso guest-houses.

The monks, together with their "husbandmen", were self-sufficient in providing their food and drink. A garden provided herbs and vegetables, an orchard fruit; cider, wine and beer were made and stored in a cellar under the control of the cellarer. There were granaries and storage houses for corn, oats, wheat and other goods. The monks had a mill on the Tweed where the present mill stands and a tenement in Bridge Street nearby was known as Almerie Land. Now Almerie refers to a storage cupboard; the Almoner distributed goods such as food and clothing to the poor from the Almonry. What better place to have the stores than alongside the mill? When building work was being carried out in Vault Square, off Mill Wynd, a cellar was found containing huge slate bins and shelving which would have been used for storage.

A doo-cot held a supply of pigeons for food but their tendency to raid grain-fields meant keeping a tight control on their numbers. Fish were held in fish-ponds before being transferred to the fisheries or brought to the table and the River Tweed at the edge of the Abbey grounds was well-stocked with salmon. The Abbot was very strict about the conservation of small fry to protect future stocks. There would have been pigsties and stables, and probably a stud for horse-breeding. Odenal d' Umfravil gave $\frac{1}{10}$ of the colts from his brood mares, which were branded and followed their dams for two years before joining the Abbey stud.

Laymen lived within the precincts of the Abbey to assist the monks and to help them to fight off any enemy. For this they were exempt from charges or dues and often received payment from the Abbot for their services.

To the North of the Abbey lay the large square cemetery, joined to the church, with a wall to keep animals out. It seems likely that this whole North side was used for burials as the former Spread Eagle Hotel in Bridge Street had a cellar known as Hardie's crypt and other nearby buildings have extensive cellars. Originally there was no road between the houses and the graveyard and in later centuries there were two entrances to the precincts of the Abbey, the Easter and Wester Kirk Styles, through which modern traffic could not pass. The Easter Kirk Style was widened by demolition of a house in 1910 and Jeffrey, in "the Antiquites and History of Roxburghshire", reports that the Wester Kirk Style had a large flight of steps which have since been levelled out. A house between these Styles is known as "the Priory". Funerals to the Abbey church passed through an iron gate into the North door.

Brewing was an extensive industry and all along Roxburgh Street are properties which once held malt steeps, barns and yards and no doubt ale-houses for thirsty travellers. This street, formerly known as the Common Way, was the well-used route between the Abbey at Easter Kelso and the ferry-crossing to Roxburgh Castle at Wester Kelso. Also known as "Faircross",

Wester Kelso was at the Floors Castle end of the present town, and its buildings were demolished early in the 18th century when the first Duke of Roxburghe extended his garden.

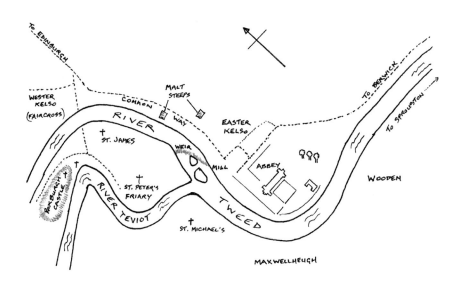

Sources:

Liber de Calchou
Thiron, Abbaye Medievale, Denis Guillemin
History and Antiquities of Roxburghshire – A. Jeffrey
Royal Commission on Ancient Monuments – H.M.S.O.
Scotland's Music – John Purser
Society of Antiquaries of Scotland, 1984
Monasteries – R. J. Unstead
Medieval Scotland – Peter Yeoman

Chapter Four

Possessions

hen David, as Earl, founded his monastery in Selkirk, he had a charter drawn up to record the details. *"An Abbey in honour of St. Mary and St. John the Evangelist, for the weal of my soul, of the souls of my father and my mother, brothers and sisters, and all of my ancestors."* The boundaries are described as *"the land of Selkirk from where a rivulet descending from the hills runs into Yarrow, as far as to that rivulet which, coming down from Crossinmara, flows into Tweed; and beyond the said rivulet which falls into Yarrow, a certain particle of land between the road which leads from the Castle to the Abbey and Yarrow, that is, towards the old town."* Ditches or *fosses* were the usual way of marking territory, with walls to enclose property. The original Abbey is believed to have been on the site now occupied by the old kirkyard at Lindean. David granted the monks the towns of Midlem, Bowden, Eildon and the lordship of Melrose, *"by the middle street and middle well, as far as the fosse, and as the fosse marches, falling into Tweed, in like manner, in lands, waters, wood and plain."*

It was the practice then for people founding religious institutions to grant them land, woods, fishings, saltworks, churches – even slaves. Although their motives were ostensibly pure, these gifts were made in exchange for the welfare of the soul and a guaranteed entry to Heaven, which, it was thought, the religious orders could procure by offering up prayers and masses. Sometimes landowners made grants to the monks in exchange for shelter within the Abbey, where they could receive instruction and pardon for their sins. Many monks worked in the countryside and knelt to pray in the fields at set times of the day. The improvements wrought by the hard work and agricultural skills of the monks brought benefits to the countryside all over Scotland. The extensive flocks of sheep under their care and the resulting wool industry were sources of wealth and employment to them and to the nation at large, with continual traffic over land and sea, particularly from the major port at Berwick.

To the Tironensian monks of Selkirk David gave land in Sprouston, Berwick and Roxburgh as well as fishings, income from the mill and burgh revenue, a percentage of cheeses from Galloway, half the (animal) skins of the kitchen and hides from deer and sheep together with a share of suet and tallow. From his property in England – at Hardingstone – he gave the mill, 24 acres of land and meadow belonging to the lordship and other land near the bridge of Northampton including an island of meadow nearby. This charter was drawn up during King Alexander's reign and Herbert's time as (3rd) Abbot and was therefore dated between 1119 and 1124.

In 1128, after two years of preparation, David transferred his Abbey foundation to Kelso *"by the advice of John, bishop of Glasgow and others of my chief men"* – possibly for the convenience of proximity to Roxburgh Castle. He reconveyed the gifts granted to Selkirk and added land at Lilliesleaf, but omitted Melrose and Eildon because these were to be conferred on the monks of the new Abbey there. The town of Tranent was gifted in place of the territory in Northampton.

The land measurements in use at the time were based on an ox and plough being driven. An oxgate/oxgang was 13 acres; two oxgates formed a husbandland; four husbandlands – a ploughgate or carucate – covered 104 acres.

The bishop of St. Andrews gifted the church of St. Mary, which already existed at Kelso, with ½ ploughgate of land, to the monastery. This land was in separate strips and therefore of lesser value, so Malcolm IV later exchanged it for a ½ ploughgate on the road to Nenthorn. Malcolm also granted the monks the church of Selkirk with a half-carucate of land *"which in the time of David lay scattered throughout the field but so that that half carucate is spread as a useful plot Malcolm gives them in the same town as much land as before but in one piece in exchange for the foresaid land."* David granted the monks 40/- annually from the revenues of the burgh of Roxburgh and 20 chalders, half of meal and half of wheat, out of the mills.

The early church of Roxburgh had been held by Ascelin, archdeacon of Glasgow, and it was only after his death that David was able to grant to the Abbey all the churches and schools of the burgh and all property belonging to them. There were three churches: The Holy Sepulchre in King Street, Old Roxburgh, attached to a prebendal (sharing revenue for occasional service) stall in Glasgow Cathedral; the church of St. John the Evangelist within the Castle with two chaplains, one a parson; and later in 1134 St. James outwith the Castle walls, which gave its name to the St. James' Fair. Herbert the

Abbot retained a portion of this land in his own hands until 1160, some time after he had become bishop of Glasgow. Two other chapels were erected near Kelso by Herbert de Maccuswel, sheriff of Teviotdale, who had inherited a 'vill' in the spot which now holds the Border Union Showground. St. Michael's was granted to the monks in 1159 and confirmed by Malcolm IV; Herbert's gift of the Oratory to St. Thomas the Martyr near Wooden was confirmed in 1232 by Robert, bishop of Glasgow, but in 1362 it was given to Thomas de Middleton by Edward III of England.

The town of Easter Kelso was gifted to the relocated monastery and from its twin town and burgh of Wester Kelso an annual rent of £9.16.9 ½ was granted together with certain duties by the freeholders. During the reign of William the Lion (1165-1214), Arnold, son of Peter of Kelso, gave the monks a messuage (i.e. a dwelling with ground attached) which had belonged to his father and some land with toft and croft; 3/- to be paid annualrent by Ralph, provost of Kelso, and his heirs. He also gave a piece of ground in town which had been the property of Walter, son of Hecke and Ingebald. In 1237 Andrew, son of William the Dyer, resigned a portion of ground which he had inherited in Kelso for 2 marks of silver paid by the Abbot. The Abbey fishings on this part of the River Tweed extended from Broxmouth (now within the estate at Floors) to Eden Water where it joins the Tweed.

At Ednam, the parish near Kelso founded in the time of David's brother King Edgar, there was a mill and David granted the Abbey a yearly income of 12 chalders of malt from it. William the Lion gave the monks three carucates of land there, the boundaries of two and a half given as: "North of Ednam petary (where turf was cut), along the boundaries of parishes on the south side of Newton (Don) and along Eden to the bridge west of Ednam, thence to the road leading to the hospital (St. Leonard's) at the forking of the road which comes from the north. Another ½ ploughgate was east of the quarry belonging to the Abbey, between 14 acres of land belonging to Pagan de Bosseville, the hospital land, the petary and the road leading to Sprouston ford".

Grants to Kelso Abbey were too numerous to list here, but a selection of various gifts and the reasons for bequest may give some idea of the source of the Abbey's great wealth. The climate in the twelfth century was relatively mild and allowed cultivation at higher altitudes than usual and for wheat to be grown at a more northerly latitude. Several grants of pasture for flocks of sheep were on high ground.

David granted the village of Redden (about 3 miles from Kelso on the south side of the Tweed) to the monks, with a grange or Abbey homestead where they could keep pasture for sheep and oxen. A grange was controlled by a lay brother or one of the monks and included storage barns for implements, byres for cattle and a granary. Outside the grange lived the cottars who occupied a hamlet or toun and paid rent with money and in kind. The farmers were obliged to provide a service by taking a horse to Berwick every week in summertime carrying weights of corn, salt or coal which were slightly reduced in the winter. Alternatively they could provide two days work a week, or three days during the harvest when they were expected to supply a waggon. John FitzHugh of Redden was said to hold land called Flooris at Selkirk belonging to Kelso Abbey "contrary to justice". On the Monday after the feast of St. Bartholomew the Apostle in 1258 he resigned it at the Abbot's Court at the bridge of Ettrick. His son Hugh sold land at Redden and Hume at the court of Abbot Richard in 1285, giving services which were later commuted for money, 19 cottages and 2 brewhouses.

Bernard de Hadden, son of Brien, gave 10 acres on the west side of the village of that name. The Abbot granted Bernard permission to have a private chapel in his mansion; the chaplain was obliged to swear fealty to the Abbot and offerings were to be given to the parish church.

At nearby Sprouston there was common pasture for 12 oxen, 4 young horses and 300 hogs (sheep), and 6 cottages. The cottage next to the vicar's house had 6 acres of land with a brew-house. An oxgate of land held by Hugh Cay brought in 10/- per annum. William de Morville, Constable of Scotland 1188-96, and his wife Muriel gave the monks 6 oxgangs of land, a toft and croft in Broxmouth and after William's death this was confirmed by Muriel and her second husband, Robert de Landeles. Galfrid de Perci gave the monks a ploughgate of land at Heiton, next to the land of the hospital (or Maisondieu) at Roxburgh.

The barony of Bowden held 28 husbandlands from the monks of Kelso, renting at Pentecost (Whitsun) and Martinmas (November). Each paid annual rent of 80 sterlings or silver pennies as well as the usual services. Each husbandman with his wife and family reaped for 4 days in autumn and with 2 men for 5 subsequent days. Each drove a wagon of peats from Gordon to the stable-yard (presumably at Kelso Abbey) for one day. Each journeyed to Berwick and received victuals en route from the Abbey. They had to provide workers for sheep-washing and shearing and carry wool from the barony to the Abbey. Four husbandmen at the ploughgate of Priestfield were bound to find men-at-arms to be leader of 30 archers raised to serve in the king's army.

Shotton and Colpinhope were actually beyond the "march" in Northumberland, but were not far from Yetholm. Robert de Schottun gave the monks 5 acres where they could dig for turf. Colpinhope, where there was a mill owned by Walter Corbet, laird of Makerstoun, and the miller, who ground the corn for the Abbey, held 3 acres of land with common pasture. At Colpinhope the monks had a "receptacle" for goods in time of danger, being very near the Border, and they used 2 ploughs for the winter season; there was pasture for 20 oxen and 20 cows, 500 ewes and 200 two-year-old sheep.

At Clifton the superior of Molle (Mow) gave the monks 7 acres for providing the communion elements. Uctred of Molle granted the church there for the good of the souls of King David and Prince Henry, with land adjacent which he and the dean had "perambulated". Henry's son William I had a natural daughter, Margaret, by the daughter of Sir Adam Hutcheson, and at Roxburgh Castle she married Eustace de Vesci who was gifted the manor of Sprouston by Royal Charter. Margaret gave land at Molle to the monks. The Abbot gave permission in 1207 for Eustace to have a private chapel. Anselm of Molle gave 8 acres of land, meadow and wood and his son Richard Scot gave another 8 acres. Anselm's daughter Matilda and her husband Richard de Lincoln confirmed the grant. The wife of Henry of Molle, Eschina de Londoniis, gave common pasture and fuel for use by the men of the monastery residing at Molle for the soul of her daughter, who was buried at Kelso. At Primside, 2 oxgangs, pasture for 1000 sheep, 24 cows and 8 oxen were granted for the soul of Prince Henry, who had given the "vill" to the father of Gaufrid Ridel. Richard Cumyn granted the church at Linton for the soul of Prince Henry and of his own son John who was also buried in Kelso Abbey. Thomas Somerville, lord of Carnwath and Linton, in 1427 granted to "God, the Blessed Mary, the Blessed Machutus, the Lord Abbot of Kelso, the Prior of St. Machutus and the monks of his church at Lesmahago"....lands lying within Linton and Hoselaw to be held in "pure alms for the offering of devout prayers".

In Berwickshire the lord of Upsettlington (Ladykirk), Robert Byseth, gave the hospital of St. Leonard at Horndean with 16 acres and fishing on the Tweed. The Abbot was to procure a chaplain of good character, a chapel and sustenance for 2 paupers. In Berwick itself, at that time in Scotland, the Kelso monks were entitled to fishings paying £20, half the profits of the mills, and annual cess from the Tolbooth of 40s. In addition, they got a dwelling with 3 shops in Uddingate and a mansion near the bridge-house for their own use. At Tweedmouth David gave a building with a well and 3 acres and Prince Henry granted a toft called Dodin's land.

Cospatric, Earl of Dunbar, and his successors of the same name, granted many churches and lands to Kelso Abbey – at Greenlaw, Lambden, Haliburton, Fogo, Hume, Mellerstain. Langton church was given for the soul of Prince Henry, with a ploughgate and land called Coleman's flat. The Church of St. Michael at Gordon, with land, was gifted by Richard de Gordon; his grandson Thomas granted land called Brun Moss with liberty to make a bridge to the petary and take timber from the woods. In return, Thomas' bones were to be buried in Kelso Abbey. His daughter Alicia married Sir Adam Gordon of Haddo and her son granted more land along the side of the Eden. The serfs who worked the land were virtually slaves and went with it. In 1280, Bernardus Fraser gave land in West Gordon along with Adam, the son of Henry de Holga his serf, "along with his whole bag and baggage".

Walter de Lindsay gave the church at Ercildoun (Earlston) with a carucate of land. The church at Cranston had been granted by Hugh Ridel for the souls of David and Henry and the profits were to be enjoyed by the secretary of the convent at Kelso. In 1316, William de Lamberton, bishop of St. Andrews, exchanged the church at Cranston and land at Preston in Midlothian for the church of Nenthorn and the chapel of Little Newton. Richard de Hanggandsyd asked the monks to pray for the souls of William and James, Earls of Douglas, and the safety of Archibald, Earl of Douglas. He granted land at Kaimflat in the territory of Little Newton bounded on the north "by the morass of Kanmuir, through which the causeway and the highway run".

The Abbey was given a Saltwork in the carse on the northern shore of the Forth by King David and another at Lochkendeloch by Roland of Galloway, son of Uctred, together with enough wood to serve the pans. David decreed that half of the skins and fat of beasts killed on the south of the Forth, all skins of rams and lambs, $1/10$ of the deer skins and cheese produced on estates in Tweeddale, and $1/10$ of cattle, swine and cheese from Galloway should belong to the monks. David's grandson Malcolm also granted the monks the right to $1/2$ the fat of any whales which might be stranded on either shore of the Firth of Forth. This arrangement was commuted by Alexander II (1214-49) for 100 shillings annually out of the feu duties and customs of Roxburgh.

In 1144, King David founded a Tironensian priory, dependent on Kelso, at Lesmahagow in Lanarkshire, which became famous for its orchards. The villa was given to the Abbey, with houses en route at Peebles and Lanark. When Prince Henry died in 1152, his father decreed that the revenues of the burgh of Peebles were to be used for masses for his soul. Henry's son William later confirmed the possession of the chapel of Peebles Castle with a ploughgate of land to the monks.

In 1159 David's grandson, Malcolm IV, granted a second charter to the monks of Kelso. He confirmed all grants made by David and added the tithes of Lilliesleaf Mill and included Whitelaw with Whitmuir at Selkirk. Besides the land originally granted to the Abbey at Selkirk, there is a half-carucate (about 52 acres) of land in the "King's Selkirk", which is the present town.

The Earl Marischal, John de Keith, had a dispute with the monks over land at Hundeby Keith (Humbie). He relinquished a portion of land lying between the monks' wood given by Simon Fraser (whose granddaughter married Hervy Keith) and a burn which ran to the church. However, the monks erected a mill and made a mill-pond there, so depriving the lords of Keith of their right to multure (fee) for milling corn grown on their lands, and they also made a road over his land. In the end, the Marischal relented and gave them liberty to have their mill and to cross his land.

When William the Lion, King of Scots, was captured at Alnwick in 1174, the English took him captive to Normandy. There were several churches gifted at that time in exchange for prayers for his safe deliverance. At Campsie his brother David, Earl of Huntingdon, gifted the church and at Closeburn the church was given for the safety of William and his son Alexander. At Pencaitland, Everard conferred the church in return for prayers for William's safety. King William himself donated the church at Dumfries and the chapel of St. Thomas. He also confirmed gifts of Stapilgorton, with land and fishery, by William de Cuniggeburc. Wilbaldington was given by Adam de Port in the presence of Robert, chaplain of Roxburgh and William, chaplain of Kelso.

In Lanarkshire, at Symington, Symon Lochard tried to claim patronage of the chapel in opposition to the monks but withdrew in their favour and his chaplain was allowed to hold the living during his lifetime. A descendant of Symon's tried to reclaim the living but was compelled to cede it and swear an oath not to molest the monks under pain of excommunication. Symon Lochard and Joceline, Abbot of Melrose, confirmed the conferring of a church at Thankerton on the Abbey by Anneis de Brus. Dunsyre Church was granted by Joceline's brother Helias.

The church at Eglismalesoks in Clydesdale was gifted to Kelso in 1321. John Lindsay was then bishop of Glasgow and he declared that the monastery, though impoverished by war, was the true patron of the church and granted it in return for the safety of the soul of Robert the Bruce.

In 1190 at Innerwick, East Lothian, four men let their portions of forest and pasture land to the monks for up to 20/- per annum. This arrangement was approved by Walter the Stewart and his son Alan confirmed a lease for 33 years and was rewarded when the monks transformed a piece of waste ground by their skill and industry.

In Edinburgh, Abbot John (1160-80) was granted a toft between the West Port and the Castle and the tenement paid the convent 16 pence per annum. The monks had been in possession of the church and lands at Easter and Wester Duddingston from the early days and Abbot Herbert granted them to Reginald de Bosco for an annual rent of 10 merks. In 1466 Abbot Allan granted land here to Cudbert Knytheson, burgess of Edinburgh.

King David's gifts to Kelso Abbey extended as far north as Aberdeenshire, where he granted them the church of Culter, in later years the subject of acrimony. The Knights Templar had been formed in 1118 when a small group of French Crusaders vowed to defend Jerusalem, recently captured from the Moslems, and were given a house near the Temple of Solomon as their base. After living off alms for 10 years, they adopted a form of Cistercian Rule, wore white cassocks with a red eight-pointed star and began to acquire numerous estates. The Order was universal, but one of their number in Scotland, Walter Byseth, built a chapel in 1221 on the Abbey's land at Culter, Aberdeenshire. He engaged "in the presence of the Abbot and monks of Kelso, assembled in full chapter, to observe all the liberties of the said church". At Lauder it was agreed that the knights should retain possession of chapel, tithes, cemetery and baptistry but should pay 8½ merks annually to the monks in the house of the Temple at Blantrodoc. A decision was made in 1287 to divide Culter in two – the part called Maryculter remained with the Knights while Peterculter stayed with Kelso Abbey. At the church Council of Vienne in 1312, the Order of Knights Templar was suppressed and their possessions passed to the Knights Hospitaller. They were still in possession of Maryculter at the time of the Reformation.

Sources:

Ednam & its Indwellers – John Burleigh
Mediaeval Scotland – R.W. Cochran-Patrick
Flower of the Forest – J. Gilbert
Old and New Edinburgh – James Grant
The History of Kelso – James Haig
The Roads of Mediaeval Lauderdale – R. P. Hardie
The History and Antiquities of Roxburghshire – Alexander Jeffrey.
Linton Leaves – J. F. Leishman

Date	King	Abbot	Event
1100	Edgar		Henry I marries Matilda (aka Edith)
1107	Alexander		David Earl in Southern Scotland
1113	"	Ralph	David founds Abbey at Selkirk
1118	"	William	Princess Matilda of England marries
			Holy Roman Emperor 1114
1124	David	Herbert	David and Queen Matilda reign
1128	"	"	Abbey moves to Kelso
1147	"	Arnold	Herbert becomes bishop of Glasgow
1152	"	"	Prince Henry buried in Kelso Abbey
1153	Malcolm IV	"	King David dies at Carlisle
1160	"	John	Malcolm subdued Galloway
1165	William I –the Lion	"	Malcolm IV died at Jedburgh
1180	"	Osbert	Independent Scottish Church
1203	"	Geoffrey	Lindores Abbey founded 1191
1206	"	Richard de Cane	King John quarrelled with the Pope
1208	"	Henry	Scotland invaded by English
1214	Alexander II	"	William had reigned 50 years
1218	"	Richard	John dead -England under Regent
1221	"	Henry de Maunsel	Marriage of Alexander II to Joanna
1239	"	Hugh	Abbot is "superior" of Kelso
1248	"	Robert	Scots/Eng. Border boundary settled
1249	Alexander III	"	New king only 8 years old
1258	"	Patrick	Henry de Lambden objected
1260	"	Henry de Lambden	Haco of Norway invaded 1263
1275	"	Richard	Henry de Lambden buried at once
1286	Interregnum	"	Scotland without a monarch
1292	John Balliol	"	Edward I dominating Scots
1296	Interregnum	"	Edward at Kelso – Abbey affected
1306	Robert the Bruce	Walron/ Thomas	Edward I died 1307
1315	"	Wm. d'Alyncrome	Battle of Bannockburn 1314
1329	David II	Wm. de Dalgernock	David taken to France
1371	Robert II	Wm. de Bolden	Alliance formed with France
1390	Robert III	"	Battle of Otterburn 1388
1398	"	Patrick	Civil war in England
1406	Regent Albany	"	Prince James captive in England
1424	James I	"	James married Joan Beaufort
1437	James II	William	New king 6 years old – regency
1460	James III	?	Coronation in Kelso Abbey
1464	"	Allan	Peace with England
1473	"	Robert	King made him commissioner
1476	"	George	Witnessed charters
1481	"	Robert	Auditor in Scots Parliament
1488	James IV	"	Border chiefs close to king
1511	"	Andrew Stewart	Commendator/Lord Treasurer
1513	James V	Thomas Ker	Flodden 1513 – country devastated
1528	"	James Stewart	Natural son of the king
1542	Mary Queen of Scots	"	Mary taken to France – regency
1545	"	"	Kelso Abbey sacked by English

Chapter Five

The Living Monastery

hen the building of Kelso Abbey began, the Tironensian monks under Abbot Herbert were transferred from Selkirk and given temporary accommodation in Roxburgh Castle. This was one of the main residences of King David I and was situated across the Tweed from Kelso, a short distance from the Abbey. Several roads led to Roxburgh, coming from all directions, some dating from Roman times. There is mention of an old stone-arch bridge which was destroyed in 1398, but whether it dated from David's time is unknown. There were certainly ferries across the Tweed in several places and these were still in use until the 19th century.

The Church of St. Mary at Kelso came under the Bishop of St. Andrews, but David obtained a measure of independence for the Abbey by arranging a grant of immunity from all tolls and services, with permission for the Abbot and monks to receive ordination and the other sacraments of the church from any bishop they pleased in Scotland or Cumbria. The "cure" of the original church of Kelso was absorbed by the abbey, served by a pensioner vicar answerable to the Abbot. Herbert would have travelled to France every three years to be present at Tiron for the Conference of Abbots from all the monasteries of that Order.

In 1147, when John bishop of Glasgow died and was buried at Jedburgh, Herbert of Kelso succeeded him, being consecrated on 24th August by Pope Eugenius III at Auxerre in France. He was replaced as Abbot of Kelso by Arnold, whose sad duty it was to conduct the burial service for Prince Henry, heir to the throne of Scotland, on 12th June 1152.

David I died the following year at Carlisle and his body was taken via Queensferry to Dunfermline for the funeral. Young Malcolm IV, David's grandson, was a boy of 11 years. King Stephen of England died in 1154 and Henry II, at 21 an older and more powerful monarch than his cousin Malcolm, ascended the throne of England. Malcolm held lands in England and for these he did homage to Henry in 1157.

1159 was the year when Malcolm's Great Charter of Confirmation ratified all grants of land to Kelso Abbey. The famous letter 'M' *(above)* at the beginning of that charter featured David and Malcolm and it is thought that the illustrators worked at Kelso Abbey. The next year the bishopric of St. Andrews became vacant and Arnold of Kelso was appointed. He was consecrated by William, bishop of Moray, Papal Legate for Scotland, in the presence of King Malcolm and many of his nobles. Arnold wrote a treatise on "The right government of a Kingdom" and presented it to the king, urging him to take a wife to assure the succession but Malcolm, known as 'the Maiden', had taken a vow to remain celibate.

John, the chanter or precentor of Kelso Abbey, became Abbot in Arnold's place and was blessed by one of his predecessors, Herbert, bishop of Glasgow. John attended the royal court and witnessed many charters and public transactions. He made one of his men, Osbern, a freeman and granted to him a ½ carrucate of land in Midlem at the annual rent of 8s. while another of his men, Walden, was given two different grants of land which incurred annual rent. John had been in post five years when Malcolm IV died and William his brother – "the Lion" – took the throne.

The Prior of Kelso at this time was Walter, who wrote *"On the Freedom of the Scottish Church"*, *"An appeal to the Court at Rome"* and *"A Collection of Letters"*. Roger, Archbishop of York, who had been appointed to act as Legate of the Roman See in Scotland, was a rival to Thomas a Becket, Archbishop of Canterbury, and had ambitions to be primate of the Scottish Church. Roger sent a haughty summons to the Scottish clergy to meet him at Norham Castle. They unanimously agreed to deny the legitimacy of his authority and sent Ingleram, bishop-elect of Glasgow, with a strong escort, to tell him of their decision. Walter, Prior of Kelso, and Solomon, Dean of Glasgow, apparently argued most eloquently but failed to shake Roger's ambition. However, he was foiled when Abbot John went to Rome and returned with a mitre, the first Abbot of a Scottish House to be so honoured. John was permitted to wear the mitre when celebrating mass in the Abbey, during processions in the cloister, and when attending the Pope's Councils.

William I granted a charter to the monks of Kelso allowing them right of market under certain restrictions. The men of the monks living in town were allowed to buy fuel, materials for building and provisions on any day except the market day at Roxburgh. They were permitted to display for sale in their own windows bread, ale and meat, and any fish they had carried to Roxburgh on horseback and brought back unsold. Dealers who passed through town with cartloads of goods would not be allowed to stop, but must carry on to Roxburgh market. William also set up a Royal Mint, supposed to be at Roxburgh although the artificers of Kelso Abbey produced coins and some may have been minted at Kelso in times of trouble. This is thought to be the origin of the "Cunzy Neuk" at the corner of the Square with Roxburgh Street.

In 1174, William I was captured in battle at Alnwick by Henry II and kept prisoner. Henry sent an avenging army into Scotland and Roxburgh was among the castles taken by the English so Kelso Abbey, still only half-finished, must have been affected by this invasion. William was taken to Falaise in Normandy and there was visited by nobles and clergy from Scotland. Arrangements were made for William to be released providing 21 Scots barons were held as hostages until the terms of a treaty could be agreed. William was obliged to do homage to Henry, making his people feudal subjects of the English king. The National Assembly in Edinburgh decreed that funds to aid the king should be raised by imposing taxes on those able to afford it, such as barons and clergy. However, the Scottish clergy refused to bow to Canterbury and Ecclesia Scoticana (Scottish Church) is mentioned for the first time.

In 1176, a dispute between John, Abbot of Kelso, and Gauthier of Tiron as to which of them was greater indicated Kelso's growing importance. Two years later King William created an Abbey at Arbroath dedicated to Thomas a Becket (who had been murdered on the orders of Henry II in 1170) and manned it with monks from Kelso. William gave the Arbroath monks a Charter of exemption from all subjection or allegience to the parent house. John quit-claimed (a deed of release) obedience to Reginald, Abbot of Arbroath, and repeated this when Reginald was followed by Henry. William's younger brother, David, Earl of Huntingdon, founded an Abbey at Lindores in Fife and this too was said to be colonised from Kelso. Abbot John died in 1180 and one plenary (i.e. complete) service was held for him in the convent with the rather puzzling comment *"as is usual for a brother who dies outside the church"*. Thirty masses were to be given by priests for his soul. John's replacement, the 4th Abbot of Kelso, was Prior Osbert of Lesmahagow who frequently witnessed charters for King and bishop.

King William had resisted the interference of Pope Alexander III in appointing a bishop to St. Andrews, despite all attempts to make him conform, so he was excommunicated and Scotland was forbidden to use the sacraments and public offices of religion. After the death of Pope Alexander in 1181, William sent Abbot Osbert, together with Joceline, Bishop of Glasgow, and Arnold, Abbot of Melrose, to Rome. Their mission to Lucius III was successful, there was reconciliation and the pontifical curses were removed. William's chaplain, Hugh, was appointed to the Metropolitan See. The new Pope sent William his paternal blessing and a sceptre of gold with rose and twig, symbolising the Rose of Sharon. The Pope conferred on Kelso the privelege that no sentence of excommunication should be enforced against them unless it came from the Apostolic See.

In 1189, Henry II of England was killed in battle, to be succeeded by his son, Richard the Lionheart. Richard's one thought was to join a Crusade. He released William the Lion (by now married to Ermengarde de Beaumont, a descendant of Henry I) from the Treaty of Falaise, returned all occupied castles in Scotland, and received payment from him of 10,000 merks in silver. To raise this money it was necessary to impose a tax in Scotland and Kelso Abbey would have been included as one of the wealthiest foundations in the Kingdom. Having regained his freedom from the English yoke, William sought to confirm the independence of the Scottish church from Canterbury or York. In his Bull Anxietatibus *of 1192, Pope Celestine declared the Scottish church "the special daughter of the apostolic see" and only subject to the pontiff.*

Celestine III died in 1198 and the following year the new Pope, Innocent III, wrote to the chapter of Kelso Abbey that churches which supported the funds for the sustenance of the Abbey, the hostel and the poor were not to be taken from the monastery by abbots and conferred on individuals, even priests. He prohibited others from injuring the monastery, suggesting that its immunities had been disregarded.

In 1201 the Bishop of Glasgow demanded that perpetual vicars should be instituted – vicars were underpaid compared to canons and challenged the settlements. Some abbots were withdrawing vicars from lands and converting them to their own use; some were receiving so much of the revenues that there was insufficient left for the vicars to be maintained. The use of hired priests was quite common.

The exact boundaries between lands granted to Kelso Abbey and to Melrose Abbey by David I became the subject of dispute in 1202. John de Salerno, apostolic legate, was asked to intervene, stayed 50 nights at Melrose and finally left, laden with gifts, having come to no conclusion. Abbot Osbert died in 1203 and was succeeded by Geoffrey as 5th Abbot. The following year at Selkirk, King William himself settled the matter of the boundaries in Kelso's favour. He confirmed the boundary which David had indicated by means of ditches running east and west on the mid hill of the Eildons. Melrose received compensation, with Kelso's agreement, of land and pasture for 400 sheep at Primside in the parish of Morebattle.

Abbot Geoffrey did not enjoy his position for long, and in 1206 Richard de Cane, the new Abbot, attended the elevation of Bricius of Douglas, Prior of Lesmahagow, who became Bishop of Moray. Meanwhile Kelso's Prior, John, was referred to the Episcopal See of Aberdeen but died the year after, shortly followed by Abbot Richard de Cane. Henry, who had succeeded John as Prior, then became the 7th Abbot.

In England, meanwhile, King John's cruel reign was in full swing. He had quarrelled with the Pope over the appointment of the archbishop of Canterbury and refused Langton, the Pope's choice, permission to land in England. Innocent III then put England under interdict and all the bishops left the country.

The bishops of Salisbury and of Rochester, at their own expense, came to Kelso for sanctuary and were well-treated by William.

King John invaded Scotland but made peace with King William when it was agreed that John should choose a consort for Alexander, William's heir. William still held lands in England and for these Alexander did homage, receiving a knighthood from John. Threatened with deposition, John submitted to the Pope in 1213 and received absolution. King William died in 1214, and his son Alexander II succeeded.

Abbot Henry travelled to Rome and he assisted at the General Council where the weighty agenda included the "deliberate extirpation of the heretic Waldensis".

In June 1215, John's unhappy subjects, supported by Alexander II, forced him to accept the Magna Carta. When John repudiated this agreement and hired mercenaries to attack his nobles, many of them fled to Scotland for protection. Alexander II travelled to Kelso and wrote to King John putting forward his family's old claim to Northumbria. He laid siege to Norham and John responded by arriving with forces to burn Berwick, reportedly setting fire to the house where he himself lodged. He burned Roxburgh Castle in February 1216 and several other towns and castles. King John died of dysentry in October that year.

In Kelso, Abbot Henry died in 1218 and was succeeded on 19th October by the Prior, Richard. He, with Walter, bishop of Glasgow and the Abbot of Melrose were the papal delegates in choosing a new Abbot for Paisley and affixed deeds to the decision. King Alexander's chamberlain, Philip de Valognes, had a son William who died and was buried at Melrose, against the wishes of the monks of Kelso. However, there was much rejoicing in 1221 when Alexander married Joanna, sister of the fourteen-year-old English King Henry III, who attended the wedding. The marriage took place at Roxburgh Castle and there was a banquet held at Kelso Abbey. By now the Abbey building was completed and it would have been at its most magnificent.

There was a dispute between the Abbot of Kelso and the bishop of Glasgow about the church of Campsie, which had been gifted when King William was in captivity. The matter was thrashed out at Roxburgh Castle and the Abbot resigned Kelso's right to the bishop. It is not clear whether this was Abbot Richard, who died that same year, or the secretary of the monastery, Herbert de Mounsel, who became 9th Abbot.

The mill at Kelso had existed since the time of William I, who granted the monks liberty to grind corn, free of multure, at Ednam if their mill at Kelso was affected by frost or flood. Now Andrew Maunsel, who owned land known as "the Halech" to the east of Roxburgh (and may have been related to Herbert) gave leave to the monks to hold in perpetuity their own mill pond on the Tweed, taking as much land as they wished in exchange for the salvation of his soul and those of his ancestors and heirs. The monks set about constructing a cauld at the right angle to create a fast flow to drive the mill wheel. Weirs in those days were constructed like stake-and-rice, or brushwood, fences and Lord Thomas de Gordon gave the monks leave to take away enough wood to build the mill pond and to repair it, providing that he was buried in the cemetery at Kelso.

It was at this time that Alexander II granted land to the Greyfriars on the opposite bank of the Tweed from the Abbey, near Roxburgh, and St. Peter's Friary was erected in 1232. The Franciscans (founded 1210) followed the example of St. Francis of Assisi , owned nothing, carried no money, walked barefoot, and moved around the countryside befriending the poor, lepers and other outcasts. Their only duty was to save souls and they received support from most of the bishops and backing from Henry III. For their true piety and dedication to learning (Duns Scotus was of their number) they were generally revered. During excavations at Springwood, the foundations of 13th century cottages were found and these may have been houses for the laymen attached to the Friary. Earlier discoveries at the Friars included a subterranean passage and a well, both built of freestone.

Despite conforming to the extent of taking the eccentric Adam of Lennox as his confessor, Alexander II maintained control over the church in Scotland by supervising appointments and allowing only token independence. Guarding his own authority in ecclesiastical matters, the king warned a visiting papal legate: "In Scotland, wild men dwell, thirsting for human blood."

The monks of the Abbey meanwhile were intending to improve the road westward over Minchmoor, which led to the Priory at Lesmahagow and continued to Glasgow, and to build a bridge over the Ettrick capable of carrying wheeled vehicles. Approval was obtained from the king, who granted about 16 acres of land which Richard, son of Edwin, quitclaimed in favour of the monks for the upkeep of the bridge.

Kelso still had control over chapels such as Roberton, Symington and Crawford-John, which wanted to gain their freedom. Crawford-John and Maryculter were the only successful ones, the latter after controversy with the Knights Templar.

In 1236, William, bishop of Glasgow, consecrated the Friary of St. Peter and a special agreement was reached with the monks of the Abbey to allow the brothers to be buried in consecrated ground beside their chapel, without prejudice to the Abbey.

This same year, on the feast of the Nativity of the Virgin, 8th September, Herbert the Abbot, now a weary old man, abandoned his charge by laying the staff and mitre on the Great Altar. Although Hugh, one of the monks, took on the duties of Abbot, the papal legate, Otho, compelled Herbert to continue until 1239, when Hugh was officially appointed 10th Abbot. Mention is made at this time of the burgh of Kelso, with the Abbot and convent as Superior, as a thriving settlement under the Abbey's protection.

After a Council at York in 1237, King Alexander gave up his claim to Northumbria and the border line between England and Scotland was roughly fixed in its present position. Queen Joanna died childless in 1238; next year Alexander remarried – to Marie de Coucy – at Roxburgh. A son, Alexander, was born there in 1241.

That same year Christiana Corbet of Makerstoun married Patrick, Earl of Dunbar and Abbot Hugh gave them permission to have a private chapel. Patrick's mother, Ada, was a natural daughter of William the Lion. The Earl gifted to the Abbey his serf Halden and his brother William and all their children and descendants.

On 27th March 1243, Kelso Abbey was dedicated by David de Bernham, bishop of St. Andrews and a year later Abbot Hugh attended King Alexander's Parliament. The Abbot and convent received authority from the Papal See to excommunicate thieves and invaders of their estates and property, and other evils directed against the church. Sentences were to be solemnly pronounced with lighted candles and ringing of bells on a Sunday or holiday and repeated annually on the Thursday before Easter (the feast of the Assumption) and other occasions. An injunction was issued by the papal legate to archdeacons, deans, parsons, vicars and chaplains requiring them to give effect to sentences of excommunication. Abbot Hugh died in 1248.

Alexander II died in 1249 when his son, the young Alexander III, was 8 years old. At that time coronations of Kings of Scots were not given the blessing of the church and Alexander II's appeal to papal authority to rectify this had been jealously opposed by Henry III. Alexander III married Margaret, daughter of Henry III of England, at York in 1251. He refused to do homage to Henry for Scotland.

Robert de Smailholm was now Abbot of Kelso and was granted a charter in 1250. Bishop David de Bernham of St. Andrews allowed the monks of Kelso to serve the church at Simprim with a chaplain instead of a vicar, contrary to vows. The Pope, also called Alexander, advised Robert the Abbot about the appointment of priests to churches that owed allegiance to the bishop. When David de Bernham was dying in 1253 he chose Kelso Abbey as his burial place rather than his own cathedral.

While Alexander III was a minor, the Earls of Menteith and Buchan, both Comyns, controlled Scotland, but in 1255 they were ousted from the regency and replaced by a Council of 15 lords chosen by Henry III who called himself "Principal Counsellor".

Henry III was invited by Alexander to stay at Roxburgh and a procession was made to Kelso Abbey for debate. Abbot Robert witnessed Alexander's proclamation, made at Roxburgh, giving the results of the conference.

In 1257, Pope Alexander wrote to the Abbot and convent giving them permission to wear scull caps, although not the custom, because several of the monks had died due to having uncovered heads during inclement weather. There was famine in Scotland at this time and the price of grain was very high. The Pope also wrote to Robert and the archdeacon of Teviotdale about a dispute at Whithorn.

Robert de Smailholm died in 1258 and was succeeded by Patrick, a monk. However, the chamberlain of the Abbey, Henry de Lambden, was very displeased and took himself off to Rome. He returned in 1260 carrying papal letters instructing Patrick to retire in Henry's favour and the former meekly obliged, placing the insignia of the Abbey on the Altar. Henry gave permission to Roland de Greenlaw to have a chapel in his house, provided no loss should accrue to the church of St. Mary in Kelso nor to the parish church. Matilda of Molle granted her thirds in the lands of Molle to the abbots and monks of Kelso, on condition that they should board and educate her son with the best boys who were entrusted to their care. Orphans were sometimes made wards of the Abbot until they came of age.

Prince Edward of England (later Edward I) visited his sister Queen Margaret at Roxburgh in 1266 and again in 1268 before he and his brother Edmund departed on an expedition to the Holy Land. King Alexander and Queen Margaret went on a visit to England and their first child, a daughter named after her mother, was born at Windsor. Two Princes, Alexander and David, followed.

It was at this time that the Sprouston Breviary was written, mainly about St. Kentigern to whom Glasgow Cathedral is dedicated and where he was buried. This consists of spoken rhymed and syllabic verse telling of Kentigern's life and also music notation for singing plainchant. The material is derived from the Salisbury rite and its chants, but the title of Sprouston suggests it may have originated near Kelso.

The monks of Melrose had possessions in Molle for which they paid tithes to Kelso Abbey. Thinking they should be exempt, they ceased payment and were sued by the Kelso Abbot for arrears of £300. In 1269, they were told to pay 260 marks for arrears and £20 for expenses. Abbot John of Lindores, sister house to Kelso, died in 1274 and was buried at Kelso Abbey. A year later, Henry of Lambden, that forceful prelate, died suddenly while eating his dinner and was buried immediately.

In 1275, Queen Margaret died at the early age of 35. Prince David died in 1281. Prince Alexander married Margaret of Flanders at Roxburgh Castle in 1283 but died a year later, and Princess Margaret, who had married the King of Norway, died in 1286, leaving an infant daughter Margaret. King Alexander realised the urgency of replacing his heir and remarried at Jedburgh Abbey in October 1285, his lovely bride Yolande de Dreux.

The 14th Abbot of Kelso, Richard, was probably invited to the wedding. William de Home was charged with harassing the monks and swore to respect their rights in future. From the land of William de Bosseville the monks received annualrent of 2/6, with 200 eggs and four days work, ground for building a house and a receptacle for fuel at the Pulles. Walter, the vicar at Wiston in Roberton, seized corn tithes which he felt were his due, but he was tried by the church authorities and judgement was given in favour of the monks of Kelso.

Disaster struck Scotland in March 1286 when King Alexander, returning to his palace in Dunfermline from Edinburgh, was thrown from his horse and killed. His infant granddaughter Margaret of Norway was declared heir to the throne. Now began years of strife and civil war, while Edward I of England exerted domination over his neighbouring kingdom, convinced of his right and invited to be arbiter by the unwary Scots. Bishop Robert Wishart of Glasgow sent two priests to Edward for guidance and in the meantime the Scots Council appointed 6 guardians to rule Scotland in Margaret's name. The main aim of the clergy was to retain the independence of the church in Scotland. Edward proposed that Margaret should be betrothed to his son Edward, the Abbots of Kelso and Melrose agreed, and all parties met at Birgham near Kelso to discuss the details. In spite of all their scheming, they were thwarted by the death of the poor princess as she sailed from Norway to her fate.

The succession to the throne of Scotland now became the focus of bitter feuding and Abbot Richard of Kelso supported John Balliol, one of the candidates. Richard was chosen as one of Balliol's commissioners to examine the various claims to the crown. On behalf of John Balliol, a document was delivered to Edward by Adam Blunt, warden of St. Peter's Friary, denying that he had supremacy in Scotland. Unfortunately, Balliol was no match for the bullying Edward I and meekly submitted to him in homage. The Border erupted and English merchants in Roxburgh and Berwick were murdered. Edward sent an army to capture Berwick, then Dunbar, and Roxburgh Castle was surrendered by James the Steward at the blast of a trumpet, without a

COMPETITORS FOR THE SCOTTISH THRONE 1296

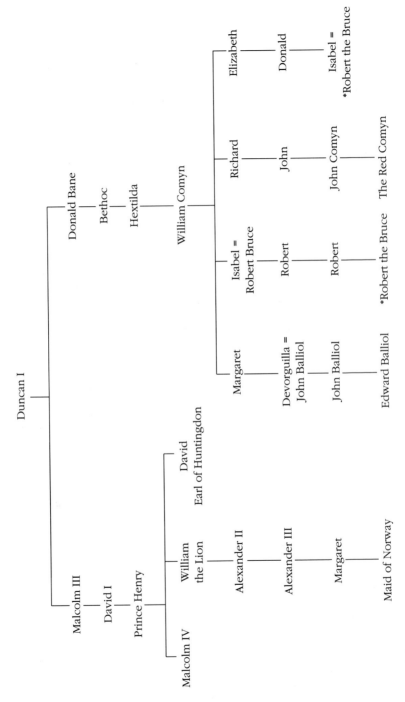

fight, on condition that all should be spared. In 1296, Edward occupied the Friary of St. Peter near the Abbey and, together with many other prelates and clergy, Richard of Kelso swore fealty to him. He was rewarded by letters, addressed to the sheriffs of Berwick and Roxburgh, ordering restitution of the estates and goods of the monastery. But things grew worse as lawless freebooters set fires indiscriminately and ravaged the Abbey. The once great, wealthy, hospitable Abbey, noted for the splendour of its rights and its boundless works of charity, was shattered. The monks and novices were forced to roam the  countryside begging for food, and shivering with cold as a mini Ice-Age began to affect the whole country, crops failing and famine resulting.

In 1300 the temporal income which Kelso Abbey derived from Roxburgh was 100 shillings from the King's revenue (presumably now Edward's) and £8.2s.9 from several tenements. From the church they received an annual pension of £13.6s.8d.

The bishop of Glasgow was confined in Roxburgh Castle and William Wallace, who now became Scotland's champion, laid siege. The Earl of Surrey, de Warenne, was governor of Scotland in Edward's absence. He arrived with a large army, relieved the siege and advanced on Kelso. Edward I visited Kelso again in 1301, when the English parliament rejected papal interference between the two countries.

In 1303 Edward gathered a great army at Roxburgh prior to marching North, and mass was celebrated before the Prince of Wales. John de Bretagne became governor of Roxburgh and Jedburgh Castles. Edward now appointed his own Abbot, Walron, to Kelso and he was followed by Thomas de Durham, who was regarded as having usurped the titles of Kelso and of Lesmahagow. He was accused of spending wastefully and embezzling the goods of both monasteries.

William Wallace and Robert Bruce restored Scotland's independence and Bruce had been crowned king the year before Edward I died in 1307. Bruce's sister Mary was confined in a cage in Roxburgh Castle until 1310. Sir James Douglas laid siege to the Castle in 1313 and captured it by dressing his men to resemble cattle grazing in the gloaming. Gradually the Scots regained their towns, castles and abbeys and after the Battle of Bannockburn in 1314 Bishop Wishart of Glasgow was released from imprisonment, a blind old man.

Bruce was not in favour with the Pope, John XXII, and two cardinals were sent to Roxburgh and two to Westminster to try to persuade the Scots to live peacably with the English, making the mistake of addressing Bruce as a nobleman rather than King. This angered Bruce who retaliated and was excommunicated, but the cardinals were unable to find a cleric to deliver the papers to him and were forced to retire. Now the Pope sided with Edward II of England in his fight against Bruce and ordered the latter to appear before him at a papal court in Avignon. As Pope John refused to recognise Bruce as King and there was a predictable reaction, the excommunication was renewed. This resulted in the Declaration of Arbroath which had such an effect on Pope John that he tried to persuade Edward to make peace with the Scots. In vain, for the English invaded Scotland but were forced to retreat when Bruce burned all before them, leaving no food for their army. In their retreat they sacked several Abbeys. Edward II was obliged to call a truce with the Scots in 1323 to last 13 years.

William d' Alyncrome was appointed Abbot in 1315 to Kelso Abbey which had suffered great hardship as a result of constant fire and plunder. He held court at Wester Kelso, complaining that the burgesses had created new burgesses, stallers and brewers without authority. The clerk to the burgesses admitted that as long as their lord, the Abbot, held the town of Kelso in his own hand, and not set in ferme (leased out), all liberties of the burgh should belong to him, provided those elected by him were presented in courts according to the laws of the burgh.

The chantry of St. James below Roxburgh was founded by Roger d' Auldton and he endowed it with £20 sterling from lands at Auldton, Heiton, West Softlaw and 6 burgages (land held of the king) in Roxburgh. The chantry was under the patronage of the Abbot and convent of Kelso, who, under peril of their souls, at the death of the chantry priest were obliged to present a successor within 2 months. Failure meant that the archdeacon of Teviotdale would be present within 6 weeks – if not, the aldermen and corporation of

Roxburgh would appoint a chaplain. In 1346, William, bishop of Glasgow, threatened with excommunication all who unjustly occupied and kept possession of the lands and liberties of the chantry of Roger d' Auldton if they did not make restitution within 15 days.

The death of Edward II in 1327 led to an invasion of England by the Scots and they laid siege to Norham. This was lifted when young Edward III offered the hand of his sister Joan as bride to Bruce's son David. The marriage took place in 1328 when David was 4 years old, his bride 7.

In the treaty between Edward III and Robert Bruce, the rights of the church in each kingdom were declared inviolate and Edward ordered that all lands and pensions which the abbeys of Kelso, Jedburgh and Melrose held in England and which had been seized by his father, should be restored.

Bruce died the following year just before the news of the Pope's decision to lift the excommunication could reach him. His heart was removed and carried on Crusade by Sir James Douglas, giving that family the right to use a heart in their crest. The boy David was crowned King, his appointed regents died, and Scotland was once more invaded by the English, bringing Edward Balliol to become King as vassal. The Battle of Halidon Hill was a dreadful defeat for the Scots.

Kelso Abbey was affected and the Abbot, William de Dalgernock, fled to Chateau Gaillard in France with the young King David, his wife and sisters and acted as tutor there. Edward Balliol acknowledged the English king as his liege lord and in 1332 he ceded the town, castle and county of Roxburgh to him. In 1333 Edward III gave letters of protection and restitution of the Abbey property and the monks were granted leave to cut wood in the forests of Selkirk and Jeddart to repair the monastery. The warden of the Abbey was now Thomas de Hassynden and Edward III granted permission to send to England for the purchase of provisions. However, the Priory of Lesmahagow was burned by the King's brother John of Eltham while people were seeking sanctuary inside. St. Peter's Friary was also occupied and Edward III paid them cash for the use of the ford at the Teviot for 205 days.

In March 1342 Roxburgh Castle was retaken by Sir Alexander Ramsay and when King David II returned to Scotland some months later, after a truce between the English and French, he was made Governor of the castle and Sheriff of Teviotdale. Ramsay's former friend Sir William Douglas, the previous sheriff, in jealousy captured him and threw him into a dungeon at remote Hermitage Castle, where he starved to death.

In 1343 David II erected Kelso, Bowden and Redden into a regality, the superiority invested in the Abbot and monastery which they retained until the Reformation. He granted to the Abbot (his erstwhile companion in exile) and monks of Kelso Abbey the enjoyment and possession of the village of Kelso with its land and pertinents. A charter was issued the following year confirming the grant giving the monks leave to cut wood in the forests of Selkirk and Jeddart to help repair the Abbey, which was badly damaged by warfare, and the upper part of the tower was renewed. The Abbey was granted the privelege of a free market and had bestowed on it the forfaultries of all rebels within the town and county of Berwick.

Instead of remaining in his own country and helping it to rebuild, David invaded England after their victory against France at Crecy. He was captured at Neville's Cross near Durham in 1346 and imprisoned in the Tower of London. The process began to raise money for his ransom, and other expenses and debts, by taxing the country. Lands were to be taxed on their real value – barons were to pay ½, clergy ³/₁₀, burghs ⅕. 23 important hostages were taken. Eustace de Lorraine, who had sworn fealty to the English king, became Warden of Roxburgh Castle. To the misery of heavy taxation was added the scourge of the Black Death. The rich shut themselves away in their castles to escape infection, the gates locked to keep the poor outside.

The infirmary of Kelso Abbey must have been the scene of many a ghastly death as Bubonic Plague – the "Black Death" – decimated the population. Many died within three days of being infected; pustules, fever, black spots, rotting flesh and congested lungs caused rapid deterioration. The corpses were so numerous that they were shovelled into pits. There was dreadful suffering as normal life ground to a halt.

In 1355, Edward III again invaded Scotland and destroyed so much by fire that it became known as Burnt Candlemas, begun on the Feast of the Purification of the Virgin. Edward Balliol at Roxburgh submitted his crown rights to Edward III and gave him a golden crown and a handful of Scottish soil as tokens.

In 1357, a treaty was made at the Friary near Roxburgh by which lands on the Border were to remain in the hands of the current possessors, so Edward III kept Roxburgh Castle. Over the next few years the Castle was completely repaired.

David II was now allowed to return to his country in exchange for 100,000 merks, only part of which was ever paid. David's wife Joan died in 1362 and he married his mistress, Dame Margaret Logie. A weak king, often in exile, David had no real feeling for Scotland and did not have the respect of his nobles, which gave rise to the Council known as The Three Estates – prelates, barons, burgesses.

Kelso Abbey appears to have continued under English jurisdiction, for their king granted the Abbey and convent protection in 1366. In 1368 a letter was addressed to the governor of Berwick: " Know ye, that as in behalf of our beloved in Christ, the Abbot and Convention of Kelso in Scotland, who are in our faith and peace – it is made known to us that the said Abbacy, its lands, tenements and possessions, as also those holding of them, are very much wasted and almost annihilated by various losses through the war, as also by various molestations, inquietudes and other losses which they are daily visited with..."

A year later, Berwick was again in English hands and David erected Dunbar as a port to replace it for export of goods by the monks and people of Teviotdale to the Continent. A truce was entered into for 14 years. Edward III granted the burgesses of Roxburgh 40 merks to repair their bridge. By now, William de Bolden (Bowden) had become Abbot of Kelso and was in post when David II died in 1371.

David's successor was his older nephew Robert, who had acted as regent at times during David's absence. Robert was the son of Walter the Steward who had married Robert Bruce's daughter Marjory and was 54 when he came to the throne. His reign was short and ineffectual, as crimes went unpunished and revenues were misappropriated. William, Earl of Douglas, was very powerful in the South of Scotland and his son married Euphemia, daughter of the king. There was constant warfare against the English who still held many Border strongholds.

In 1371, at the annual fair of Roxburgh which seems to have continued through all the fighting, a member of the Earl of March's household was killed by the English. This led to years of animosity between March and the Earl of Northumberland, with incursion of each other's territory, burning and killing. It reached a climax in 1377, when the Scots fought with courage and overcame their enemies at the "Bloody Fair of Roxburgh" but set fire to the town. Edward III was succeeded that year by his grandson, Richard II, who granted protection to the monks of Kelso, their convent and lands.

In England John Wyclif, whose followers were known as Lollards, began a dissenting movement which carried influence among the clergy. Three English clerics fled to Scotland and the Bishop of Durham, Walter Skirlaw, directed the archdeacon of Northumberland to apprehend James Notyngham, John Wythby and Robert de Roxburgh.

The French and Scots had formed an alliance in 1372 and the former came to Scotland in 1385 to uphold it, but were poorly received. A joint raid into England was unsuccessful but in retaliation the English under Richard II invaded and burned the Abbeys at Melrose, Dryburgh and Newbattle, but not Kelso.

The French returned home but the Scots went on to fight and win a battle called Otterburn (or Chevy Chase) against 'Hotspur' Percy. A truce was called in 1389 and King Robert II died the next year. His lame son John became king, taking the title Robert III, but failed to control his unruly and powerful brothers. One of them, the Duke of Albany, had been Governor under his father and continued under Robert III until his powers were taken from him. Robert was so inept that the General Council transferred power in 1399 to his son David, Duke of Rothesay.

At Kelso, the new Abbot was Patrick, who gave a pension of 2 marks from farms at Midlem to Richard de Hanggandsid. He also granted to a priestly monk licence to study any liberal science or permissable art for two years at either of the English universities, and to choose a confessor.

It is interesting to note that an agreement to try to reach a lasting peace between nations involved the meeting of commissioners to resolve any grievances. The complaints of the Scots were to be sent to Roxburgh Castle, but those of the English were to be sent to Kelso. One of the complaints made by the English was against the Earl of Douglas and Sir William Stewart for breaking down the bridge of Roxburgh.

England was in the throes of civil war, for Richard II was challenged by Henry of Lancaster and eventually imprisoned in the Tower of London. When Richard died in 1400, apparently from self-imposed starvation, Henry IV became king. Two years later David, Duke of Rothesay, also died and his uncle Albany again became Governor of the Realm. Border warfare broke out anew and men changed loyalties with bewildering speed. To save his eldest surviving son James from Albany's power, Robert III sent him by sea to France, but the ship was captured by the English and the wretched monarch died of grief. Now the way was clear for Albany, regent in the absence of the heir to the throne, and he proved an able ruler, which is more than could be said for his son Murdoch who succeeded him in 1420. Murdoch was beheaded by James I, King of Scots, who returned from England in 1424.

The Abbot of St. Andrews disputed the right of precedency claimed by the Abbot of Kelso over all the other abbots of the kingdom, in consequence of priveleges conferred upon them by David I, the Holy See and others. James I presided over a full discussion before Parliament and decided in favour of St. Andrews, assigning to them the precedency of all Abbots on the grounds that the monastery of St. Andrews had been the first erected in Scotland.

Henry IV of England had died in 1413 and Henry V in 1422 and the new King Henry VI was an infant. James King of Scots married Joan Beaufort, niece of Henry IV, the year he returned to Scotland, promising to pay 60,000 merks for his "board and lodging" during his captivity and not to ally with the French against the English.

In 1428, Abbot William of Kelso notified Pope Martin V that a chantry which had been founded in the parish of St. James at Roxburgh by Roger d' Auldton for the celebration of Mass on behalf of himself and his family had been discontinued because of the destruction of the church and its property in the recent wars. The Pope gave permission, with the consent of the rector of the church and the heirs of the founder, to transfer the service to a convenient chapel in his Abbey until St. James' could be repaired.

James I asserted his right to appoint bishops without interference from the Pope and stopped his churchmen bargaining with Rome as it gave away the influence of one of the Estates of the kingdom. Aeneas Sylvius Piccolomini, who later became Pope Pius II, visited Scotland, describing James as a robust and excessively fat man while his common subjects lived in abject poverty. James arranged a marriage between his daughter Margaret and the Dauphin of France and when she was en route she was almost captured by the English, as he had been.

In revenge for this action, in 1436 James besieged Roxburgh Castle which was still in English hands, but abandoned the assault prematurely when his Queen arrived with a warning of a conspiracy against his life. Another William was now Abbot of Kelso.

In 1437 James I was stabbed to death and his six-year-old son, who had a flaming birth-mark on his face, was crowned James II in Holyrood Abbey. James II married Mary of Gueldres in 1449. In England Henry VI was declared insane and Richard, Duke of York, became regent. Henry recovered but war broke out between houses of York and Lancaster. James II took Henry's side, probably because his mother's family the Beaufort Dukes of Somerset were Henry's supporters.

James II besieged Roxburgh Castle in 1460, bringing his artillery to the opposite bank of the Tweed near the house of Floors. His main cannon, the Lion, exploded and he was mortally injured. He was taken to the Friary of St. Peter, where he died of his wounds. His son, a boy of 9 years, was crowned James III in Kelso Abbey, one of the most momentous events in its history. It is reported that the Abbey had not been visited by superiors for a hundred years because of the English occupation – the number of monks had by now dwindled to 17. The widowed Queen urged the army to continue their assault on Roxburgh Castle, which fell to the Scots forces and was destroyed.

Henry VI of England and his wife, Margaret of Anjou, were exiled in Scotland and Berwick was restored to the Scots. Edward of York took the English throne. The Dowager Queen Mary and Bishop Kennedy acted as regents on behalf of James III and the bishop continued when Mary died in 1463.

Allan was Abbot of Kelso Abbey from 1464 for two years. He granted 2 lands (tenements) on the north side of Castlegate in Jedburgh to John Rutherford of Hundalee and his wife Elizabeth in return for housing the Kelso Abbot or monks free of charge during visits to Jedburgh. Allan also let property at Mellerstain to Alexander and Hugh Purves for 19 years. William de Hattely, son of Robert, gave the monks permission to build a bridge over the rivulet at Blakeburn and to have a road to the "petary".

James III married Margaret of Denmark and the islands of Orkney and Shetland were ceded to Scotland as her dowry. James began to govern in person in 1469 and he concluded a treaty with Edward IV.

In 1473 Robert was made Abbot of Kelso and was directed by the king to treat with the English commissioners about the redress of grievances in the Borders. Lawless people of either nation who failed to recognise the truce were to be punished. At Edinburgh Abbot George witnessed a crown charter of James III to the church of Glasgow in 1476 and two years later he was sent to escort the almoner of Edward IV from the Tweed to Edinburgh. His successor, another Robert, sat in the Scots Parliament, appointed by the Three Estates as Lord Auditor of causes and complaints. The Abbot of Kelso took precedence, the Abbot of Melrose second place. One of the Kelso monks of this time, James, was a celebrated Scottish author, a man of sound judgement and a skilled mathematician. Abbot Robert's signature appeared on a vellum charter in July 1481 in favour of Ellen, wife of Walter Ker of Cessford, and their son, Robert, heir to lands in Bowden.

War again broke out on the Border in 1481, with Richard of Gloucester supporting James III's brother, Albany, and marching into Scotland with an army supplied by Edward IV, who reckoned he had been promised homage, land and castles. Berwick was retaken for the last time. The Scots barons were jealous of some of the king's favourites and while James was with his force at Lauder, the barons attacked these men and hanged them from a bridge above the Leader. James was made prisoner by his own nobles and taken to Edinburgh Castle, but soon released. The exiled Earl of Douglas returned but was captured and sent to Lindores Abbey to live as a monk. After the death of his queen in 1486, James became grasping and demanded the revenues of Coldingham Priory, annoying the Homes who laid claim for themselves.

The practice of electing their own superiors had now generally fallen into disuse in monastic communities. In 1487 the king obtained a mandate from the Pope to direct the monks to choose an individual nominated by him. This led to the selection of secular priests, unqualified to preside over a monastery, being granted the superiority and the revenues. Bishops ordained men who were unskilled in music, some not even understanding Gregorian chant.

James, in desperate need of friends, went to Lindores Abbey and offered Douglas his freedom in exchange for support, but was rejected. His son Prince James, aged 15, was among the rebels, many of them Borderers, who fought him at Sauchieburn near Stirling in 1488. James IV always wore an iron belt as a penance for his involvement in his father's death, but the Homes and Hepburns were given office and Walter Ker became Esquire to James. The Earl of Angus was replaced as Chancellor by the king and in resentment allied himself to Henry VII of England and became his "pensioner". Apparently he was plotting to sell Hermitage Castle to England, but was detected in time and the King forced him to exchange properties with Patrick Hepburn. In 1489 Angus was directing several of the Kers at Kelso.

Perhaps this has some connection with Henry's grant in 1490 of special letters of protection and licence to the Abbot and convent of Kelso, including the town of Kelso, Redden, Sprouston, Wester Softlaw and the Barony of Bowden; all their lands, tenants, servants, corn, cattle and goods. Licence was granted to one or two monks to go with their servants into England

and buy lead, wax, wine and other merchandise for the use of the convent. They could also go to the Wardens of the Marches and demand restitution of their goods.

In 1491 there was an Anglo-Scottish truce at Coldstream but James entered into a secret agreement with France. A new Archbishop of Glasgow was created that year. The Archbishop of St. Andrews was replaced by Alexander, eldest illegitimate son of James IV.

In August 1495, under the Great Seal and Charter, Walter Ker of Cessford was granted the town of AuldRoxburgh as a free barony in recognition of the hospitality and lodging provided by him to travellers in the South Marches of the kingdom at his own expense. This was done at Stirling and the witnesses included Robert, Archbishop of Glasgow; Archibald, Earl of Angus; Lord Douglas, Chancellor; John, Lord Drummond, Justiciar; George, Abbot of Paisley, treasurer; and George, Abbot of Dunfermline. Five years later, Ker was given the castle and castlested of Roxburgh with rights over the Maisondieu. The reddendo (service to a Superior) was to be one red rose at the feast of St. John the Baptist. Six swans were sent to King James by the Abbey.

Education was made compulsory in Scotland in 1496. Parliament ordered all barons and freeholders to put their eldest sons to school aged 8-9. The monks were recognised as excellent teachers and their school at Kelso was well-used.

James IV married in 1503 Margaret Tudor, daughter of Henry VII of England who was constantly plotting against James. Henry died in 1509 and was succeeded by Margaret's brother Henry VIII, who supported the Pope in 1511 when the Holy League was formed. Sir Robert Ker of Cessford, Warden of the Middle Marches, chief cup-bearer to James IV and Master of his Ordnance, was killed by three Englishmen in 1511 and the lack of just punishment caused ill-feeling on the Border.

Andrew Stewart, bishop of Caithness, was made Commendator of Kelso Abbey, granted in trust when he was appointed Lord High Treasurer of Scotland.

Henry VIII invaded France on 30th June 1513 and on 22nd August James crossed the Border into England and took Norham Castle. On 9th September the two armies met at Flodden with disastrous results for the Scots. King and nobles "the Flower of Scotland" were all slain, including James' son Alexander, Archbishop of St. Andrews.

The night after Flodden, Kelso Abbey was assaulted by Sir Andrew 'Dand' Ker of Ferniehirst, the Abbot was turned out of the monastery and Dand's brother Thomas installed.

James V was an infant in the power of his mother and her new husband, Archibald Douglas, Earl of Angus. Francis I of France sent the exiled John Stewart, Duke of Albany, to Scotland as Regent.

Albany arrived in Kelso to decide what measures to take to prevent frequent murders and robberies and he heard complaints made against the Earl of Angus and Lord Home who were tormenting the district. It is recorded that Albany imprisoned the Abbot of Kelso in Dunfermline.

Margaret Tudor took refuge in the nunnery at Coldstream. She was collected by Lord Dacre and taken to Harbottle, where her daughter Margaret was born. The Earl of Home and his brother were beheaded and in revenge the Warden of the East March, a Frenchman called Sieur de la Bastie, was murdered by Home of Wedderburn. He then killed the Prior of Coldingham.

Alexander Gordon, Earl of Huntly, who had taken part at Flodden, had a son John who died en route from France to Scotland in 1516 and his body was brought to Kelso for burial in the Abbey. Thomas Ker was made Commendator on 2nd December 1517. This was the year that John Duncan, cleric of Glasgow, made his report on the monastery of Kelso. He described it as double – not only having a convent but also a ministry. The Abbot appointed a vicar to supervise the "cure of souls" over a wide parish but exercised episcopal and temporal jurisdiction over his parishioners himself. The town of Kelso had approximately 60 dwellings and nearly all the inhabitants were husbandmen and cultivators of the fields belonging to the monastery. None paid tithes or dues because the Abbot paid them to protect the Abbey in time of attack. At that time, the Abbot, Prior and Superior were usually in the cloister, which was partially unroofed due to warfare, and there were around 36-40 monks in residence.

In 1520 the Abbot was given a commission to meet with Lord Dacre, Warden of the English Marches, at Heppethgate on College Water, Northumberland, and conclude a truce until the following January. The Abbot of Kelso and Ker of Cessford met the English Warden at Redden and the truce was continued until June.

By Albany's arrangement, 4,000 French troops were sent to Scotland and massed on the Border with 28 cannons and 4 double cannons to harass Henry VIII but the Scots felt they were fighting France's war and did not want another Flodden. Henry rejected offers of a truce and ordered all Scots and French to be imprisoned, their goods seized, the men marked with a cross and sent home to Scotland.

Lords Dacre and Ross pillaged and burned Kelso in July 1522 but appear to have spared the Abbey on that occasion. Later in the year, the Earl of Northumberland wrote to Henry VIII stating that his brother Clyfforthe had advised that Kelso should be burnt, with all the corn, to prevent any garrison near the Border but luckily this was not carried into effect.

In February 1523 George Ker, canon of Glasgow and prebendary of AuldRoxburgh, willed and ordained that his executors should erect and found a chapel in the Kirk of the Blessed Virgin Mary (the Abbey) in honour of St. Salvator and Blessed Mary of Pity. As chaplain of his chapel he choose Sir John Chepman. He ordained that the old images should be burnt at the said altar and three were to be repainted: the larger image of St. Salvator, one of the Salutation of the Blessed Mary and one of St. John the Baptist. George Ker also ordained that the choir of the Blessed Mary of Roxburgh should be rebuilt and painted, given a chalice and a vestment of black with a gold fringe – the same to apply to the kirks at Morebattle and Lindean.

The Abbot of Kelso wrote to the Dowager Queen Margaret asking her to intercede with the English commander to spare the town and Abbey. She responded but her letter was ignored, for Lord Dacre marched on Kelso again under Surrey, sacked the town, gutted the monastery, demolished the Gatehouse, fired the dormitories and completely unroofed the Abbey, stripping lead and leaving the walls open to the elements and in a state of decay. The cells were burned and the vaults destroyed. They reduced the Abbot's house and surrounding buildings to ashes. The Chapel of the Blessed Virgin Mary, which had some beautiful Episcopal stalls, was ruined. The monks were forced to disperse to nearby villages where they celebrated divine worship and lived in poverty. Religious services were interrupted and the monks scattered, begging and seeking shelter.

The Earl of Surrey went on to devastate the Border. Albany now returned to France and complaints received no redress. Angus advanced over the Border causing further chaos in spite of becoming Warden of the East and Middle Marches. He still had custody of young King James V and on July 26th 1526 at Melrose Walter Scott of Buccleuch attacked forces guarding James. Although Ker of Cessford, an Angus supporter, was killed by one of Buccleuch's men, James remained with Angus.

The Abbot of Kelso assisted in concluding a truce for three years. The Abbey was still in use for legal transactions carried out before the altars and oaths were taken on the Gospel. Records mention the servant of St. Salvator (George Ker's bequest) in the monastery of Kelso during business between John Achesone and William Ker of Selkirk when the former was buying land. In 1527, Thomas Forest paid yearly 2 equal portions of 20 shillings Scots at Whitsunday and Martinmas at the altar of St. Salvator. Next year, Selkirk men were paying ferme to Sir John Chepman, chaplain for service to the altar of Our Saviour in Kelso Abbey. There was mention of lands in Selkirk belonging to "the venerable father Thomas Ker, Abbot of Kelso and convent of the same", including the "Miller's Acres". Hellen Fallaw of Softlaw was selling land to Andrew Ker who "binds himself faithfully to touch the the Holy Evangell to seal"...set to pay at the altar of St. Katrin in the monastery of Kelso.

James V took control as king in 1530 and tried to subdue the Border in a punishing series of supervised Justice Ayres – Johnnie Armstrong was hanged. Promising to defend the seat of Rome and Holy Kirk, James received the Pope's permission to draw an annuity of £10,000 from the Church for the maintenance of a College of Justice, 15 salaried clerics and laymen, learned in law and acting as supreme civil court. Bishops and Abbots offered £1,400 with a lump sum of £72,000. The tax was raised by evicting many tenants and bringing in others at higher rents. This incited hostility towards the clergy just at the time they were needing support.

Following the death of Abbot Thomas Ker in 1528, James Stewart, illegitimate son of James V and Elizabeth Shaw of Sauchie, was made Commendator of Kelso and Melrose. Young James was a pupil of George Buchanan and his lifestyle appears to have been lavish, according to accounts which list servants, a Spanish skin coat, velvet bonnet and harnessing furnished with black velvet. Three more of James' natural sons were made Commendators: Robert at Holyrood, John at Coldingham and James (later Earl of Moray) at St. Andrew's Priory. His son Adam was made Prior of Charterhouse. The king suggested to the Pope that, in order to supplement the revenues of the monasteries, the administrators for his sons should be allowed to donate tithes to them for 19 years.

Henry VIII had married Anne Boleyn and declared himself Supreme Head of the Church in England. James V persuaded one of the cardinals that the bad influence of heretical sermons being preached by the English could spread into Scotland because of the common language. He maintained that to grant to his sons the small monasteries on the Border, which were adjacent to some of the English strongholds, could check this evil. Despite all the hostilities, James received the Order of the Garter from Henry in 1535. By Act of Parliament, the English designated a large house and courtyard in Whitehall as Scottish territory on behalf of James V as Henry's nephew, to enable him to have a residence during ambassadorial visits to London. This became known in later years as Scotland Yard.

At Kelso Abbey meanwhile, there were court cases featuring the Ker family. Agreement was reached between Robert Ker and James Mather and his spouse Marion Learmont if the former would pay the cost of a lawsuit in court before the baillies of Kelso. James Ker, of Brigheuch at Selkirk, was tenant of lands there belonging to the Abbey, enclosed by a huge dyke. Ker broke through the dyke and ploughed and tilled land in the middle of the commonhaugh. This, and other violations by the Kers, was discovered during the Riding of the Marches and they were summoned by the community. Provost James Muthag of Selkirk, with baillie James Keir, rode out a third time to obtain the proof required but they were murdered. Four years later Robert Ker, now a burgess of Edinburgh, came to an agreement with Christian Murray, relict of Thomas Murray of Bowhill, leasing land belonging to her from the monastery of Kelso. She resigned all future rights.

King James married in 1537 but his bride died and he married again in 1538 – to Mary of Guise. Both dowries brought a great deal of money into Scotland. David Beaton was made a Cardinal in 1539. Henry VIII made attempts to influence James against him and to seize church property as he had done. 1541 was a dreadful year for James V. In April, his two infant sons by Mary of Guise died. In October his mother, Margaret Tudor, died at Holyrood. Henry demanded that James meet him at York but the Scots refused to let him take the risk. Henry's forces crossed the Border and were defeated by Huntly at Haddonrig in Teviotdale. The English led a reprisal by burning Roxburgh and Kelso. James died in 1542, just after the birth of his daughter Mary. Henry demanded that the infant princess be betrothed to his son Edward, but the Scots refused. The mighty thundering of Henry's wrath swept all before it.

Despite the destruction of Kelso Abbey, part of the building was still in use and when the army of the regent Arran visited Kelso the ladies and gentlemen of the district were charged to muster at the Abbey. Fiddlers played, the gunners drank from the church silver, their guns and artillery standing alongside.

Arran was a weak man, constantly vacillating between religions. He made Beaton Archbishop of Glasgow, but later imprisoned him, leading to further destruction of the abbeys by mobs who believed that his downfall implied permission. When the clergy refused to christen or bury the populace while he was in captivity, Arran released Beaton and joined the Catholic faction again himself.

In 1544, garrisons from Wark, Cornhill, Bamburgh, Fenton and Ford invaded Kelso led by Eure, Bowes and Laiton, surprised the inhabitants, killed 40 people and took prisoners. They took 100 oxen and 50 horses and drove them to the ruins of Roxburgh Castle, owned by Ker of Cessford; they took his goods, cattle, oxen, horses and mares and used the Castle as a stable and pen while their army lay in the cornfields by Old Roxburgh. A Scots army gathered under Ker of Cessford, Dand Ker of Littledean, Hume of Cowdenknowes, Scott, laird of Buccleuch and men of Ettrick Forest. They were pursued by the English, several were killed and Mark Ker was wounded but escaped. The following May, Andrew Ker, brother of Cessford, was stationed at Kelso with a garrison to defend the town and neighbourhood. His force was also pursued by the English, overtaken at Frogden and he and 30 others taken prisoner.

A decisive victory was won at Ancrum Moor by the Scots in February 1545 but in September the Earl of Hertford invaded Scotland with 12,000 men, resting at Wark and then proceeding along the side of the Tweed to Kelso. The river was in flood and several carts and horses were overthrown during the crossing. The Earl of Cumberland, Lord Scrope, Sir Robert Bewes, Warden of the Middle Marches, Lord Latimer and other knights led an army which included 300 Italians and Albanese on horseback. There were Spaniards and Irishmen and the Master of Ordnance had 100 followers. With this huge gathering, it was not surprising that food was running short. On the 9th, the Abbey was attacked and entered and although it was defended to the death by monks and laymen, by midnight the Spaniards had won it by force. The following day steps were taken to fortify the Abbey but decided against before noon. The idea was abandoned for several reasons; a number of stone buildings clustered round the Abbey would make fortification complicated; the Tweed tended to flood and would prevent victuals being brought in; Maxwellheugh provided an attacking position for the Scots; the ground was sandy and gravelly and not good for building. Roxburgh Castle would be easier to fortify, so Lord Hertford decided to transfer there. Orders were given to undermine the towers and other strong parts of the Abbey and demolish them. A few days later, it was razed and ruined – houses, towers, steeples, particularly the East end where the Great Altar stood. Lead from the roof was taken to Wark by the cartload, time after time. Three Scots were hanged in the camp and nine were killed in the fields, but in return the Scots killed three Italians who strayed from the rest. Kelso town was burnt and St. Peter's Friary ruined before the camp moved to Roxburgh Mains and then on to Jedburgh. In 1547 an English captain called Bulmer found work for his soldiers in building a guard-house at the Friary, roofing over part of the church as a stable.

When Eure again attacked Kelso, the Abbey was defended by 30 footmen but they were overwhelmed. The garrisons of Cornhill, Norham and Wark made for Nenthorn with 100 men, while the rest lay in ambush among the broom at Spittal (Berrymoss). They seized and slew 110 Scots. After they had gone, sixteen Scotsmen built a fort in the steeple of the Abbey, but it was all too late to save the magnificent edifice. The remaining portion stands sentinel to remind us of our loss.

Sources:

Liber de Calchou
The Medieval Church in Scotland – Ian B. Cowan
History of Kelso – James Haig
The Roads of Mediaeval Lauderdale – R. P. Hardie
History & Antiquities of Roxburghshire – Alexander Jeffrey
Selkirk Protocol Books – Maley & Elliot
The Forgotten Monarchy of Scotland – Michael of Albany
Kelsae – Alistair Moffat
The Lion in the North – John Prebble
Scotland's Music – John Purser
Scotland – Robert S. Rait
Society of Antiquaries of Scotland

Chapter Six

The Ruined Abbey

The preacher George Wishart was killed in 1546, Cardinal Beaton murdered three months later and John Knox was sent to France as a galley-slave. Henry VIII died in 1547, leaving his 10-year-old son Edward as King of England. Protector Somerset (formerly Earl of Hertford) won a battle at Pinkie, near Musselburgh, in September and travelled south.

omerset's army marched into Kelso to find the town was deserted, the Abbey in ruins, but the fortified steeple was still defended by 16 men. With him came 6,000 men, 800 musketeers, 15 pieces of artillery and 1,000 wagons and a camp was set up at the Friars. He fortified Roxburgh Castle and left a garrison there. Local families including the Kers submitted to him. Mary of Guise, as Regent, appealed to her native France for help and 7,000 Frenchmen, Germans and Italians arrived in Scotland.

In 1550 Somerset was arrested and the Duke of Northumberland became Protector. The English withdrew from Scotland but the French stayed on for another 8 years. Mary Tudor became Queen of England in 1553 and restored Catholicism to her country, causing many refugees to cross the Border. Mary of Guise tolerated Protestantism but promoted her own religion in Scotland, although the Reformation and John Knox were powerful forces against her.

Mary of Guise accompanied an army to Kelso under the command of the Earl of Arran and they were joined by French artillery provided by M. d'Oysel, the French Ambassador. They crossed the Tweed and camped at Maxwellheugh before moving on to Wark. Kelso was put in a state of defence and a garrison was left there by Lord James Stewart (later Earl of Moray), half-brother to the Commendator.

When James Stewart, Commendator of Kelso, died in 1558, the Abbey remained in the hands of the Crown. Regent Mary made her brother Cardinal Guise Commendator of Kelso and Melrose, but he didn't reap any revenue

In 1825

Kelso Abbey Looking West

In 1925

N.B. Note the high tower which has appeared!

for the following year monachism was suppressed in Scotland by the Lords of the Congregation. They took the Abbey in the name of the Crown, drove out the remaining monks and a mob destroyed the furnishings – even the library wasn't spared. The damaged buildings were repaired at great expense to the new Commendator.

Elizabeth became Queen of England in 1558 and Mary of Guise died in 1560. The Reformation gathered pace and hearing Mass was forbidden, under severe penalties. Some nobles claimed that their ancestors had gifted lands to the Church and they were entitled to reclaim them. A compromise was reached whereby the value of the benefices was to be given up to the State, the incumbents were to get 2/3 and the other 1/3 would be annexed to the Crown.

There had been a tradition of education by the monks of Kelso but this could not continue as before. The Book of Discipline of 1560 made education compulsory and a Grammar School was established in Kelso, occupying part of the loft of the ruined Abbey – a fairly primitive affair with rushes on the floor, where the boys lay to write on their slates.

Shortly before his death in 1564, Brother Henry Cant of St. Peter's Friary, with consent of other brothers, granted a charter to Walter Ker of Cessford of the lands belonging to the Friars of Roxburgh. The Kers occasionally used the Friary as their residence, and the 2nd Earl of Roxburghe entertained the King's High Commissioner there in 1669. They bought the rights to run the ford and ferries across the Teviot and this continued until the bridge was built in 1794. There was a productive farm on the site until the 1840s but there is now no sign of the Friary, remembered only in the name Friarshaugh, a course for point-to-point races.

Sir John Maitland was briefly Commendator of Kelso but the town had no religious leader until Adam Clark was appointed "exhorter" (unqualified preacher) to Kelso and Nisbet. In 1565, there was a Charter by the Commendator "with assent of his Chapter regularly assembled, in favour of Mark and Thomas Ker of Yair, in consideration of their services, seisen of the lands of Kippilaw within the Barony of Bowden and the regality of Kelso, to be held by them as feu and heritage forever on payment of a yearly sum of money and certain services." These would pass to the crown on the death of the last family representative.

Sir John Maitland exchanged the Commendatorship of Kelso Abbey for that of Coldingham which was inherited in 1563 by the infant Francis Stewart, son of John Stewart, a natural son of James V, and Janet Hepburn, sister of the Earl of Bothwell. Francis was only four years old when he became Commendator of Kelso.

This was a turbulent time in Scotland and treachery was rife. Mary, Queen of Scots had returned from France in 1561 and married Darnley in 1565. After the murders of Riccio and Darnley, Mary leaned on Bothwell but he was unpopular and Home, Buccleuch and Ker formed a confederation against him.

On 22nd August 1566 the Abbot of Kelso, William Ker, was killed by his kinsman, Walter Ker of Cessford, warden of the Middle March, who supported the Reformation.

Mary Queen of Scots visited Kelso to hold a council in November 1566 after her memorable stay in Jedburgh, with her court and 1,000 horsemen. James Stewart, Earl of Moray, (below) was half-brother to Mary and after her flight to England in 1568 he became Regent.

Moray arrived in Kelso in April 1569 and made a proclamation at the Mercat Cross in Faircross (Wester Kelso) about lawlessness. People bound themselves to the new king James VI and the Earl of Moray to resist rebellious people and thieves and agreed that none of them would harbour rebels or give any support or victuals. A bond was drawn up and signed by 33 knights from the surrounding area. That same year, Moray obtained from his nephew Francis Stewart (aged 6) and his administrator William Lumisden, rector of Cleish, a grant to him and his heirs the whole estates of the Abbey of Kelso, comprehending the town, many lands, fishings and property in 4 shires, confirmed by a Charter under the Great Seal. The next year Moray was murdered and the Earl of Lennox, grandfather of James VI, became regent with English support. Mary, exiled Queen of Scots, had adherents among the Border clans including the Kers of Ferniehirst and the Scotts. The English, under Surrey and Baron Hunsdon, warden of the East March, held a rendezvous at Kelso to counter them.

After the murder of Lennox, the Earl of Morton took merciless control of the country and for reasons of expediency revived the offices of Archbishop, Abbot and Prior and made himself nominal protector of the clergy. These offices were to draw the revenues of the Abbey lands and hand the major part to lay patrons. Ministers were starved and other people took their livings.

John Knox died and his nephew Paul, son of William Knox, minister of Cockpen, became Kelso's first Reformed minister. His kirk was formed from part of the Abbey ruin and his living quarters were below. He only stayed 2 years and was followed by John Howie. By this time only two of the original monks survived – James Ancrame and Thomas Symsone. There were rumours of Catholic revival and a mob again attacked the Abbey in 1580 when Alexander Thorntoun was minister.

The Earl of Morton was executed in 1581; the Ruthven Raid may have been an attempt to prevent James VI from becoming too close to the Catholic Church.

Minister of the kirk for twenty years from 1585 was William Balfour. In 1587, Maitland, now Chancellor of Scotland, was again Commendator with full rights to feus, taxes and rents as the last of the monks had died. All abbacies in Scotland had been annexed to the Crown but Ker of Cessford had originally been granted the "rights of an heritable baillie" by the Abbot and this continued.

When James VI returned from Denmark with his bride they were caught in storms at sea and Francis Stewart, now Earl of Bothwell, was blamed for causing them by witchcraft and his estates at Kelso were forfeited. The townspeople were accused of "treasonable reset" for the Earl and had to find security of not more than 2,000 silver merks. James pardoned them but they had to pay 1,700 merks and agree not to communicate with Bothwell under penalty. The temporality of the Abbey was annexed to the Crown in 1594, five years before James published the *Basilikon Doron* asserting the Divine Right of Kings. The revenues of Kelso with Lesmahagow were by now considerably less than at the time of the Reformation: £1,983.17s.8d money; 3 chalders of wheat; 30 chalders, 11 bolls and 2 firlots of bere; 57 chalders 14 bolls of oats; 8 bolls of meal.

On the baptism of Prince Charles in 1602, James VI created Robert Ker of Cessford a peer as Lord Roxburghe and he levied customs as feudal superior in place of the Abbot when Kelso Abbey was erected into a temporal lordship for him. He went to London with James on his accession to the English throne and in 1616 he was made Baron Ker of Cessford and Caverton and Earl of Roxburghe. He and his heirs were given power to admit burgesses and to appoint bailies and other officers in 1634 when Kelso was made a free Burgh of Barony, shedding its ecclesiastical status.

Robert Ker 1st Earl of Roxburghe.

James Knox, a nephew of Paul, succeeded Balfour as minister, also using the vaults below the Abbey as a manse. He continued until 1633 when his son Robert became minister and converted two of the Abbey galleries for house-room. Life must have been rather difficult for him when General Leslie arrived in Kelso in 1639 with his Covenanting army and set up H.Q. and a barracks in the Abbey, with entrenchments all round. Montrose himself arrived in September 1645, invited by the Kers, before his defeat at Philiphaugh.

In 1649 an attempt was made to repair another part of the Abbey ruin to convert it into a cavernous church. The east wall of the church was built in alignment with the east piers of the West Crossing, while the vestry extended east into what had been the nave. Two low and gloomy arches were thrown over the walls and another over the head of the cross, while a wing of rough masonry of vault-like character was erected in the ruined choir. A second tier of arches was thrown over the first, to serve the purpose of an outer prison which connected by a small door with an inner prison. The cell in which the church had been was then used for smuggled goods, a stable and a lumber-house before being cleared out. A series of cells extended to the south and included the aisle of Dr. Stuart's family in the 18th century.

Robert Knox was imprisoned in Edinburgh in 1654 for praying for King Charles II while Cromwell's forces occupied Scotland. Richard Waddell was the first minister after the Restoration of the Monarchy in 1660.

In 1668 the Grammar School was housed in a building attached to the north side of the Abbey and a scholars' loft was erected above that of the merchants in the church. On Sundays the boys met at school and were examined in the Scriptures before being marched to church, the rector leading the way and the doctor at the rear.

James Lorimer was minister from 1683 for four years and was therefore faced with the dilemma of the accession of James VII who favoured Catholicism. He was also witness to the disastrous fire of 1684 which swept through Easter Kelso, but ironically did not reach the ruined Abbey. Lorimer was followed by James Gray who was deposed for refusing to pray for King William (of Orange). It was at this time that a scandalous scene is recorded in the church, still part of the Abbey. A weaver from Yetholm was leading the Presbyterian faction, while the Episcopal faith was favoured by the schoolmaster, James Kirkwood. When a psalm was announced these two men selected different tunes – "Stilt" and "London" – and the peace was shattered. The minister took control by hitting the schoolmaster on the head and snatching his hymnbook, which caused laughter among the congregation. Some worshippers rushed out of the church while officers from the English regiment under Sir John Lannier cried out "The people are all gone mad and the Devil's in the minister".

William Jack filled the post until 1706 when Rev. James Ramsay arrived. Ramsay had originally been Episcopalian but bowed to pressure under

William's regime and turned Presbyterian. Kelso was again the centre of dissent in 1715 when a Jacobite force led by Mackintosh of Borlam and his Highlanders marched in to muster with Lord Kenmure. Mr. Paton, a non-juring minister, preached in the Abbey from a text in Deuteronomy "The right of the first-born is his". After the service the company marched to Wester

Print of Kelso Abbey by John Slezer, reproduced by kind permission of The National Library of Scotland. The Grammar School is on the left, the Parish Church has a sloping roof and the Jail above has a thatched roof.   (below) As it is today.

Kelso with bagpipes, drums and flying colours. These activities were regarded as treason and the commissioners of Oyer and Terminer sat at Kelso to enquire into them in 1718. The Jacobite forces of Bonnie Prince Charlie arrived in 1745 and Ramsay defused any potential trouble.

When Ramsay died in 1749 the Duke of Roxburghe selected the new minister, Cornelius Lundie, causing uproar at this interference and a split in the congregation. Lundie was minister in 1770 when a prophecy by Thomas the Rhymer that "the church would fall when at the fullest" was apparently to be fulfilled when a piece of masonry fell off the roof, and the congregation refused to return. A new Parish Church was built in the old Abbey graveyard and opened for worship in 1771. The Abbey precincts were now used as a workshop by wheelwrights, Neil and Trotter, who made the first thrashing-mills. A new Grammar School was erected in 1780 where the Abbey Row Community Centre now stands.

It is reported that around this time a very large coffin was found and opened to reveal a human skeleton surrounded by ancient relics. The bones fell to dust on exposure to the air. The coffin was on view at the Abbey before being moved to a fountain-head a mile from Kelso for use as a cattle-trough!

In 1805 William, the 4th Duke of Roxburghe, arranged for the unsightly appendages to be cleared away from the Abbey buildings. His successor in 1816 continued this work when it was discovered that the fabric was ready to fall. In 1822, noblemen and gentlemen of the county met together and employed Mr. Gillespie, (who later added Graham to his name) Edinburgh architect, to survey the ruins. His preliminary report was laid before the heritors of Kelso in November and immediate steps were taken to remove the bells from the north front of the Abbey under the supervision of the Kelso architect, William Elliot. The full report was read to a gathering of the gentry in January 1823 as follows:

"First, it appears to me from minute inspection, that unless a very speedy remedy be applied, a large portion of the building is in danger of falling to the ground; and that the bells should be immediately taken down, as I am satisfied they have been the cause of much injury to the building.

Second, that as the greatest injury the building in general has sustained appears to arise from water penetrating through the summit, and passing to the heart of the walls, all the loose stones should be fixed, the rents and crevices on the top carefully pinned and filled up and then a coat of Roman cement, one inch in thickness, should be applied for the protection of the whole upper part of the Abbey.

Third, that many of the arches and other parts of the building which are in a very crazy state, should be strengthened; and that other repairs, which it is impossible fully to specify in writing, should be executed; and that the commencement of these necessary repairs should not be deferred longer than the month of April next."

Mr. Gillespie offered his services free and subscriptions were raised to fund the repairs, estimated at £1,500, and a committee appointed to administer it. The repairs were carried out and a railing erected around the ruins to preserve it from public intrusion.

The map of 1823 shows Abbey House which had been built in the Abbey grounds and was then occupied by the Smith family and the chambers of Smith and Robson, Writers to the Signet. It was the residence of Dr. Thomas Rutherford until his death in 1911 and demolished to make way for the War Memorial, designed by Sir Robert Lorimer, which was erected in 1921, by which time the Abbey was in the care of H. M. Ministry of Works.

In April 1824, the *Kelso Mail* carried a report that workmen levelling ground within the Abbey precincts had found a fragment of a bell shaped like a wedge from which it was calculated that the diameter must have been nearly 6 feet and the weight 1 ½ tons. Also found in a mass of stones were human skeletons, the remains of leaded latticed windows with glass shards attached and a considerable quantity of charred wood.

For centuries, by tradition, the Roxburghe family had been buried at in a vault at Bowden Kirk, but when the 7th Duke died in 1892 he was buried in the south transcept of Kelso Abbey. The architect Reginald Fairlie was commissioned to design a new Memorial Cloister which was built to the south of the Abbey ruin, incorporating a 13th century doorway. The 8th Duke was buried there in 1932 and other family members have since joined him in the hallowed ground of Kelso's heritage, beneath the silent bell-tower.

Abbey House.

Sources:

Border Memories – W. R. Carre
History of Kelso – James Haig
Kelso Records – Mason
History of the Barony of Broughton – John Mackay
The Lion in the North – John Prebble
Scotland – Robert Rait
Annals of a Border Club – Tancred
History of Kelso Parish Church – Dr. J. Trainer

The photograph of the portrait of 1st Earl of Roxburghe is reproduced by kind permission of the Duke of Roxburghe.

Acknowledgements

Many people have contributed towards this account of Kelso Abbey, some perhaps unawares! The whole project began in response to a request from staff at the Tourist Information Centre in Kelso to provide a brief account of the Abbey's history on behalf of enquiring visitors who were unable to find one.

In particular I must thank:

David Welsh who established links with Thiron-Gardais and introduced me to Denis Guillemin, author of a fine book about the mother abbey at Tiron (now Thiron-Gardais) in Perche, France.

Denis, Laetitia and M. Lionel Bellina, then Mayor of Thiron-Gardais, who gave us generous hospitality during our visit in September 2000. Denis has been very helpful in his comments and kindly provided several pictures and a plan of Tiron Abbey.

Mrs. Anne Scott who not only gave permission to use a photograph of the stained- glass panel, executed by her late husband R. Macdonald Scott, for the cover but painstakingly read the draft of this book.

Ann and David Grainger, friends in Pembrokeshire, who gave enthusiastic help in finding out facts about St. Dogmaels Abbey and taking photographs.

Ian Abernethy of Heiton who investigated the history of church organs in mediaeval times and gave useful references.

Matilda Hall of Morebattle who supplied me with most helpful notes on the existence of many relevant records which would be invaluable to an in-depth researcher.

Alistair Innes for his help and advice in the art of digital photography.

Rory McDonald of the Archeology section at Scottish Borders Council who gave some expert advice and encouragement.

And my long-suffering husband Denys, who travelled with me to France and supported me throughout the project, as always.

Index